Learning Probabilistic Graphical Models in R

Familiarize yourself with probabilistic graphical models through real-world problems and illustrative code examples in R

David Bellot

BIRMINGHAM - MUMBAI

Learning Probabilistic Graphical Models in R

First published: April 2016

Production reference: 1270416

Published by Packt Publishing Ltd.
Livery Place
35 Livery Street
Birmingham B3 2PB, UK.

ISBN 978-1-78439-205-5

www.packtpub.com

Credits

Author
David Bellot

Reviewers
Mzabalazo Z. Ngwenya
Prabhanjan Tattar

Acquisition Editor
Divya Poojari

Content Development Editor
Trusha Shriyan

Technical Editor
Vivek Arora

Copy Editor
Stephen Copestake

Project Coordinator
Kinjal Bari

Proofreader
Safis Editing

Indexer
Mariammal Chettiyar

Graphics
Abhinash Sahu

Production Coordinator
Nilesh Mohite

Cover Work
Nilesh Mohite

About the Author

David Bellot is a PhD graduate in computer science from INRIA, France, with a focus on Bayesian machine learning. He was a postdoctoral fellow at the University of California, Berkeley, and worked for companies such as Intel, Orange, and Barclays Bank. He currently works in the financial industry, where he develops financial market prediction algorithms using machine learning. He is also a contributor to open source projects such as the Boost C++ library.

About the Reviewers

Mzabalazo Z. Ngwenya holds a postgraduate degree in mathematical statistics from the University of Cape Town. He has worked extensively in the field of statistical consulting and has considerable experience working with R. Areas of interest to him are primarily centered around statistical computing. Previously, he has been involved in reviewing the following Packt Publishing titles: *Learning RStudio for R Statistical Computing*, Mark P.J. van der Loo and Edwin de Jonge; *R Statistical Application Development by Example Beginner's Guide*, Prabhanjan Narayanachar Tattar; *Machine Learning with R*, Brett Lantz; *R Graph Essentials*, David Alexandra Lillis; *R Object-oriented Programming*, Kelly Black; *Mastering Scientific Computing with R*, Paul Gerrard and Radia Johnson; and *Mastering Data Analysis with R*, Gergely Darócz.

Prabhanjan Tattar is currently working as a senior data scientist at Fractal Analytics, Inc. He has 8 years of experience as a statistical analyst. Survival analysis and statistical inference are his main areas of research/interest. He has published several research papers in peer-reviewed journals and authored two books on R: *R Statistical Application Development by Example*, Packt Publishing; and *A Course in Statistics with R*, Wiley. The R packages gpk, RSADBE, and ACSWR are also maintained by him.

www.PacktPub.com

eBooks, discount offers, and more

Did you know that Packt offers eBook versions of every book published, with PDF and ePub files available? You can upgrade to the eBook version at www.PacktPub.com and as a print book customer, you are entitled to a discount on the eBook copy. Get in touch with us at customercare@packtpub.com for more details.

At www.PacktPub.com, you can also read a collection of free technical articles, sign up for a range of free newsletters and receive exclusive discounts and offers on Packt books and eBooks.

https://www2.packtpub.com/books/subscription/packtlib

Do you need instant solutions to your IT questions? PacktLib is Packt's online digital book library. Here, you can search, access, and read Packt's entire library of books.

Why subscribe?

- Fully searchable across every book published by Packt
- Copy and paste, print, and bookmark content
- On demand and accessible via a web browser

Table of Contents

Preface

Probabilistic graphical models is one of the most advanced techniques in machine learning to represent data and models in the real world with probabilities. In many instances, it uses the Bayesian paradigm to describe algorithms that can draw conclusions from noisy and uncertain real-world data.

The book covers topics such as inference (automated reasoning and learning), which is automatically building models from raw data. It explains how all the algorithms work step by step and presents readily usable solutions in R with many examples. After covering the basic principles of probabilities and the Bayes formula, it presents Probabilistic Graphical Models(PGMs) and several types of inference and learning algorithms. The reader will go from the design to the automatic fitting of the model.

Then, the books focuses on useful models that have proven track records in solving many data science problems, such as Bayesian classifiers, Mixtures models, Bayesian Linear Regression, and also simpler models that are used as basic components to build more complex models.

What this book covers

Chapter 1, Probabilistic Reasoning, covers topics from the basic concepts of probabilities to PGMs as a generic framework to do tractable, efficient, and easy modeling with probabilistic models, through the presentation of the Bayes formula.

Chapter 2, Exact Inference, shows you how to build PGMs by combining simple graphs and perform queries on the model using an exact inference algorithm called the junction tree algorithm.

Chapter 3, Learning Parameters, includes fitting and learning the PGM models from data sets with the Maximum Likelihood approach.

Chapter 4, Bayesian Modeling – Basic Models, covers simple and powerful Bayesian models that can be used as building blocks for more advanced models and shows you how to fit and query them with adapted algorithms.

Chapter 5, Approximate Inference, covers the second way to perform an inference in PGM using sampling algorithms and a presentation of the main sampling algorithms such as MCMC.

Chapter 6, Bayesian Modeling – Linear Models, shows you a more Bayesian view of the standard linear regression algorithm and a solution to the problem of over-fitting.

Chapter 7, Probabilistic Mixture Models, goes over more advanced probabilistic models in which the data comes from a mixture of several simple models.

Appendix, References, includes all the books and articles which have been used to write this book.

What you need for this book

All the examples in this book can be used with R version 3 or above on any platform and operating system supporting R.

Who this book is for

This book is for anyone who has to deal with lots of data and draw conclusions from it, especially when the data is noisy or uncertain. Data scientists, machine learning enthusiasts, engineers, and those who are curious about the latest advances in machine learning will find PGM interesting.

Conventions

In this book, you will find a number of text styles that distinguish between different kinds of information. Here are some examples of these styles and an explanation of their meaning.

Code words in text, database table names, folder names, filenames, file extensions, pathnames, dummy URLs, user input, and Twitter handles are shown as follows: "We can also mention the `arm` package, which provides Bayesian versions of `glm()` and `polr()` and implements hierarchical models."

Any command-line input or output is written as follows:

```
pred_sigma <- sqrt(sigma^2 + apply((T%*%posterior_sigma)*T, MARGIN=1,
FUN=sum))
upper_bound <- T%*%posterior_beta + qnorm(0.95)*pred_sigma
lower_bound <- T%*%posterior_beta - qnorm(0.95)*pred_sigma
```

 Warnings or important notes appear in a box like this.

 Tips and tricks appear like this.

Reader feedback

Feedback from our readers is always welcome. Let us know what you think about this book—what you liked or disliked. Reader feedback is important for us as it helps us develop titles that you will really get the most out of.

To send us general feedback, simply e-mail feedback@packtpub.com, and mention the book's title in the subject of your message.

If there is a topic that you have expertise in and you are interested in either writing or contributing to a book, see our author guide at www.packtpub.com/authors.

Customer support

Now that you are the proud owner of a Packt book, we have a number of things to help you to get the most from your purchase.

Downloading the example code

You can download the example code files for this book from your account at http://www.packtpub.com. If you purchased this book elsewhere, you can visit http://www.packtpub.com/support and register to have the files e-mailed directly to you.

You can download the code files by following these steps:

1. Log in or register to our website using your e-mail address and password.
2. Hover the mouse pointer on the **SUPPORT** tab at the top.
3. Click on **Code Downloads & Errata**.
4. Enter the name of the book in the **Search** box.
5. Select the book for which you're looking to download the code files.
6. Choose from the drop-down menu where you purchased this book from.
7. Click on **Code Download**.

You can also download the code files by clicking on the **Code Files** button on the book's webpage at the Packt Publishing website. This page can be accessed by entering the book's name in the **Search** box. Please note that you need to be logged in to your Packt account.

Once the file is downloaded, please make sure that you unzip or extract the folder using the latest version of:

- WinRAR / 7-Zip for Windows
- Zipeg / iZip / UnRarX for Mac
- 7-Zip / PeaZip for Linux

Errata

Although we have taken every care to ensure the accuracy of our content, mistakes do happen. If you find a mistake in one of our books—maybe a mistake in the text or the code—we would be grateful if you could report this to us. By doing so, you can save other readers from frustration and help us improve subsequent versions of this book. If you find any errata, please report them by visiting http://www.packtpub.com/submit-errata, selecting your book, clicking on the **Errata Submission Form** link, and entering the details of your errata. Once your errata are verified, your submission will be accepted and the errata will be uploaded to our website or added to any list of existing errata under the Errata section of that title.

To view the previously submitted errata, go to https://www.packtpub.com/books/content/support and enter the name of the book in the search field. The required information will appear under the **Errata** section.

Piracy

Piracy of copyrighted material on the Internet is an ongoing problem across all media. At Packt, we take the protection of our copyright and licenses very seriously. If you come across any illegal copies of our works in any form on the Internet, please provide us with the location address or website name immediately so that we can pursue a remedy.

Please contact us at copyright@packtpub.com with a link to the suspected pirated material.

We appreciate your help in protecting our authors and our ability to bring you valuable content.

Questions

If you have a problem with any aspect of this book, you can contact us at questions@packtpub.com, and we will do our best to address the problem.

1
Probabilistic Reasoning

Among all the predictions that were made about the 21st century, maybe the most unexpected one was that we would collect such a formidable amount of data about everything, everyday, and everywhere in the world. Recent years have seen an incredible explosion of data collection about our world, our lives, and technology; this is the main driver of what we can certainly call a revolution. We live in the Age of Information. But collecting data is nothing if we don't exploit it and try to extract knowledge out of it.

At the beginning of the 20th century, with the birth of statistics, the world was all about collecting data and making statistics. In that time, the only reliable tools were pencils and paper and of course, the eyes and ears of the observers. Scientific observation was still in its infancy, despite the prodigious development of the 19th century.

More than a hundred years later, we have computers, we have electronic sensors, we have massive data storage and we are able to store huge amounts of data continuously about, not only our physical world, but also our lives, mainly through the use of social networks, the Internet, and mobile phones. Moreover, the density of our storage technology has increased so much that we can, nowadays, store months if not years of data into a very small volume that can fit in the palm of our hand.

But storing data is not acquiring knowledge. Storing data is just keeping it somewhere for future use. At the same time as our storage capacity dramatically evolved, the capacity of modern computers increased too, at a pace that is sometimes hard to believe. When I was a doctoral student, I remember how proud I was when in the laboratory I received that brand-new, shiny, all-powerful PC for carrying my research work. Today, my old smart phone, which fits in my pocket, is more than 20 times faster.

Therefore in this book, you will learn one of the most advanced techniques to transform data into knowledge: **machine learning**. This technology is used in every aspect of modern life now, from search engines, to stock market predictions, from speech recognition to autonomous vehicles. Moreover it is used in many fields where one would not suspect it at all, from quality assurance in product chains to optimizing the placement of antennas for mobile phone networks.

Machine learning is the marriage between computer science and probabilities and statistics. A central theme in machine learning is the problem of inference or how to produce knowledge or predictions using an algorithm fed with data and examples. And this brings us to the two fundamental aspects of machine learning: the design of algorithms that can extract patterns and high-level knowledge from vast amounts of data and also the design of algorithms that can use this knowledge — or, in scientific terms: learning and inference.

Pierre-Simon Laplace (1749-1827) a French mathematician and one of the greatest scientists of all time, was presumably among the first to understand an important aspect of data collection: data is unreliable, uncertain and, as we say today, noisy. He was also the first to develop the use of probabilities to deal with such aspects of uncertainty and to represent one's degree of belief about an event or information.

In his *Essai philosophique sur les probabilités* (1814), Laplace formulated an original mathematical system for reasoning about new and old data, in which one's belief about something could be updated and improved as soon as new data where available. Today we call that Bayesian reasoning. Indeed Thomas Bayes was the first, toward the end of the 18th century, to discover this principle. Without any knowledge about Bayes' work, Pierre-Simon Laplace rediscovered the same principle and formulated the modern form of the Bayes theorem. It is interesting to note that Laplace eventually learned about Bayes' posthumous publications and acknowledged Bayes to be the first to describe the principle of this inductive reasoning system. Today, we speak about Laplacian reasoning instead of Bayesian reasoning and we call it the Bayes-Price-Laplace theorem.

More than a century later, this mathematical technique was reborn thanks to new discoveries in computing probabilities and gave birth to one of the most important and used techniques in machine learning: the probabilistic graphical model.

From now on, it is important to note that the term **graphical** refers to the theory of graphs — that is, a mathematical object with nodes and edges (and not graphics or drawings). You know that, when you want to explain to someone the relationships between different objects or entities, you take a sheet of paper and draw boxes that you connect with lines or arrows. It is an easy and neat way to show relationships, whatever they are, between different elements.

Probabilistic Graphical Models (PGM for short) are exactly that: you want to describe relationships between variables. However, you don't have any certainty about your variables, but rather beliefs or uncertain knowledge. And we know now that probabilities are the way to represent and deal with such uncertainties, in a mathematical and rigorous way.

A probabilistic graphical model is a tool to represent beliefs and uncertain knowledge about facts and events using probabilities. It is also one of the most advanced machine learning techniques nowadays and has many industrial success stories.

Probabilistic graphical models can deal with our imperfect knowledge about the world because our knowledge is always limited. We can't observe everything, we can't represent all the universe in a computer. We are intrinsically limited as human beings, as are our computers. With probabilistic graphical models, we can build simple learning algorithms or complex expert systems. With new data, we can improve those models and refine them as much as we can and also we can infer new information or make predictions about unseen situations and events.

In this first chapter you will learn about the fundamentals needed to understand probabilistic graphical models; that is, probabilities and the simple rules of calculus on which they are based. We will have an overview of what we can do with probabilistic graphical models and the related R packages. These techniques are so successful that we will have to restrict ourselves to just the most important R packages.

We will see how to develop simple models, piece by piece, like a brick game and how to connect models together to develop even more advanced expert systems. We will cover the following concepts and applications and each section will contain numerical examples that you can directly use with R:

- Machine learning
- Representing uncertainty with probabilities
- Notions of probabilistic expert systems
- Representing knowledge with graphs
- Probabilistic graphical models
- Examples and applications

Machine learning

This book is about a field of science called machine learning, or more generally artificial intelligence. To perform a task, to reach conclusions from data, a computer as well as any living being needs to observe and process information of a diverse nature. For a long time now, we have been designing and inventing algorithms and systems that can solve a problem, very accurately and at incredible speed, but all algorithms are limited to the very specific task they were designed for. On the other hand, living beings in general and human beings (as well as many other animals) exhibit this incredible capacity to adapt and improve using their experience, their errors, and what they observe in the world.

Trying to understand how it is possible to learn from experience and adapt to changing conditions has always been a great topic of science. Since the invention of computers, one of the main goals has been to reproduce this type of skill in a machine.

Machine learning is the study of algorithms that can learn and adapt from data and observation, reason, and perform tasks using learned models and algorithms. As the world we live in is inherently uncertain, in the sense that even the simplest observation such as the color of the sky is impossible to determine absolutely, we needed a theory that can encompass this uncertainty. The most natural one is the theory of probability, which will serve as the mathematical foundation of the present book.

But when the amount of data grows to very large datasets, even the simplest probabilistic tasks can become cumbersome and we need a framework that will allow the easy development of models and algorithms that have the necessary complexity to deal with real-world problems.

By real-world problems, we really think of tasks that a human being is able to do such as understanding people's speech, driving a car, trading the stock exchange, recognizing people's faces on a picture, or making a medical diagnosis.

At the beginning of artificial intelligence, building such models and algorithms was a very complex task and, every time a new algorithm was invented, implemented, and programmed with inherent sources of errors and bias. The framework we present in this book, called probabilistic graphical models, aims at separating the tasks of designing a model and implementing algorithm. Because it is based on probability theory and graph theory, it has very strong mathematical foundations. But also, it is a framework where the practitioner doesn't need to write and rewrite algorithms all the time, for algorithms were designed to solve very generic problems and already exist.

Moreover, probabilistic graphical models are based on machine learning techniques which will help the practitioner to create new models from data in the easiest way.

Algorithms in probabilistic graphical models can learn new models from data and answer all sorts of questions using those data and the models, and of course adapt and improve the models when new data is available.

In this book, we will also see that probabilistic graphical models are a mathematical generalization of many standard and classical models that we all know and that we can reuse, mix, and modify within this framework.

The rest of this chapter will introduce required notions in probabilities and graph theory to help you understand and use probabilistic graphical models in R.

One last note about the title of the book: *Learning Probabilistic Graphical Models in R*. In fact this title has two meanings: you will learn how to make probabilistic graphical models, and you will learn how the computer can learn probabilistic graphical models. This is machine learning!

Representing uncertainty with probabilities

Probabilistic graphical models, seen from the point of view of mathematics, are a way to represent a probability distribution over several variables, which is called a joint probability distribution. In other words, it is a tool to represent numerical beliefs in the joint occurrence of several variables. Seen like this, it looks simple, but what PGM addresses is the representation of these kinds of probability distribution over many variables. In some cases, many could be really a lot, such as thousands to millions. In this section, we will review the basic notions that are fundamental to PGMs and see their basic implementation in R. If you're already familiar with these, you can easily skip this section. We start by asking why probabilities are a good tool to represent one's belief about facts and events, then we will explore the basics of probability calculus. Next we will introduce the fundamental building blocks of any Bayesian model and do a few simple yet interesting computations. Finally, we will speak about the main topic of this book: Bayesian inference.

Did I say Bayesian inference was the main topic before? Indeed, probabilistic graphical models are also a state-of-the-art approach to performing Bayesian inference or in other words to computing new facts and conclusions from your previous beliefs and supplying new data.

This principle of updating a probabilistic model was first discovered by Thomas Bayes and publish by his friend Richard Price in 1763 in the now famous *An Essay toward solving a Problem in the Doctrine of Chances*.

Beliefs and uncertainty as probabilities

Probability theory is nothing but common sense reduced to calculation

*Théorie analytique des probabilités,
1821. Pierre-Simon, marquis de Laplace*

As Pierre-Simon Laplace was saying, probabilities are a tool to quantify our common-sense reasoning and our degree of belief. It is interesting to note that, in the context of machine learning, this concept of belief has been somehow extended to the machine, that is, to the computer. Through the use of algorithms, the computer will represent its belief about certain facts and events with probabilities.

So let's take a simple example that everyone knows: the game of flipping a coin. What's the probability or the chance that coin will land on a head, or on a tail? Everyone should and will answer, with reason, a 50% chance or a probability of 0.5 (remember, probabilities are numbered between 0 and 1).

This simple notion has two interpretations. One we will call a **frequentist** interpretation and the other one a **Bayesian** interpretation. The first one, the frequentist, means that, if we flip the coin many times, in the long term it will land heads-up half of the time and tails-up the other half of the time. Using numbers, it will have a 50% chance of landing on one side, or a probability of 0.5. However, this frequentist concept, as the name suggests, is valid only if one can repeat the experiment a very large number of times. Indeed, it would not make any sense to talk about frequency if you observe a fact only once or twice. The Bayesian interpretation, on the other hand, quantifies our uncertainty about a fact or an event by assigning a number (between 0 and 1, or 0% and 100%) to it. If you flip a coin, even before playing, I'm sure you will assign a 50% chance to each face. If you watch a horse race with 10 horses and you know nothing about the horses and their rides, you will certainly assign a probability of 0.1 (or 10%) to each horse.

Flipping a coin is an experiment you can do many times, thousands of times or more if you want. However, a horse race is not an experiment you can repeat numerous times. And what is the probability your favorite team will win the next football game? It is certainly not an experiment you can do many times: in fact you will do it once, because there is only one match. But because you strongly believe your team is the best this year, you will assign a probability of, say, 0.9 that your team will win the next game.

The main advantage of the Bayesian interpretation is that it does not use the notion of long-term frequency or repetition of the same experiment.

In machine learning, probabilities are the basic components of most of the systems and algorithms. You might want to know the probability that an e-mail you received is a spam (junk) e-mail. You want to know the probability that the next customer on your online site will buy the same item as the previous customer (and whether your website should advertise it right away). You want to know the probability that, next month, your shop will have as many customers as this month.

As you can see with these examples, the line between purely frequentist and purely Bayesian is far from being clear. And the good news is that the rules of probability calculus are rigorously the same, whatever interpretation you choose (or not).

Conditional probability

A central theme in machine learning and especially in probabilistic graphical models is the notion of a conditional probability. In fact, let's be clear, probabilistic graphical models are all about conditional probability. Let's get back to our horse race example. We say that, if you know nothing about the riders and their horses, you would assign, say, a probability of 0.1 to each (assuming there are 10 horses). Now, you just learned that the best rider in the country is participating in this race. Would you give him the same chance as the others? Certainly not! Therefore the probability for this rider to win is, say, 19% and therefore, we will say that all other riders have a probability to win of only 9%. This is a conditional probability: that is, a probability of an event based on knowing the outcome of another event. This notion of probability matches perfectly *changing our minds intuitively* or updating our beliefs (in more technical terms) given a new piece of information. At the same time we also saw a simple example of Bayesian update where we reconsidered and updated our beliefs given a new fact. Probabilistic graphical models are all about that but just with more complex situations.

Probability calculus and random variables

In the previous section we saw why probabilities are a good tool to represent uncertainty or the beliefs and frequency of an event or a fact. We also mentioned the fact that the same rules of calculus apply for both the Bayesian and the frequentist interpretation. In this section, we will have a first look at the basic probability rules of calculus, and introduce the notion of a *random variable* which is central to Bayesian reasoning and the probabilistic graphical models.

Sample space, events, and probability

In this section we introduce the basic concepts and the language used in probability theory that we will use throughout the book. If you already know those concepts, you can skip this section.

A **sample space** Ω is the set of all possible outcomes of an experiment. In this set, we call ω a point of Ω, a **realization**. And finally we call a subset of Ω an **event**.

For example, if we toss a coin once, we can have heads (H) or tails (T). We say that the sample space is $\Omega = \{H,T\}$. An event could be I get a head (H). If we toss the coin twice, the sample space is bigger and we can have all those possibilities $\Omega = \{HH,HT,TH,TT\}$. An event could be I get a head first. Therefore my event is $E = \{HH,HT\}$.

A more advanced example could be the measurement of someone's height in centimeters. The sample space is all the positive numbers from 0.0 to 10.9. Chances are that none of your friends will be 10.9 meters tall, but it does no harm to the theory. An event could be all the basketball players, that is, measurements that are 2 meters or more. In mathematical notation we write in terms of intervals $\Omega = [0,10.9]$ and $E = [2,10.9]$.

A **probability** is a real number $Pr(E)$ that we assign to every event E. A probability must satisfy the three following axioms. Before writing them, it is time to recall why we're using these axioms. If you remember, we said that, whatever the interpretation of the probabilities that we make (frequentist or Bayesian), the rules governing the calculus of probability are the same:

- For every event E, $P(E) \geq 0$: we just say that probability is always ~~positive~~ *nonnegative* $P(\Omega) = 1$, which means that the probability of having any of all the possible events is always 1. Therefore, from axiom 1 and 2, any probability is always between 0 and 1.

- If you have independent events E_1, E_2 ... then $P\left(U_{i=1}^{\infty}E_i\right) = \sum_{i=1}^{\infty} P(E_i)$.

Random variables and probability calculus

In a computer program, a variable is a name or a label associated to a storage space somewhere in the computer's memory. A program's variable is therefore defined by its location (and in many languages its type) and holds one and only one value. The value can be complex like an array or a data structure. The most important thing is that, at any time, the value is well known and not subject to change unless someone decides to change it. In other words, the value can only change if the algorithm using it changes it.

A random variable is something different: it is a function from a sample space into real numbers. For example, in some experiments, random variables are implicitly used:

- When throwing two dices, X is the sum of the numbers is a random variable
- When tossing a coin N times, X is the number of heads in N tosses is a random variable

For each possible event, we can associate a probability p_i and the set of all those probabilities is the **probability distribution** of the random variable.

Let's see an example: we consider an experiment in which we toss a coin three times. A sample point (from the sample space) is the result of the three tosses. For example, HHT, two heads and one tail, is a sample point.

Therefore, it is easy to enumerate all the possible outcomes and find that the sample space is:

$$S = \{HHH, HHT, HTH, THH, TTH, THT, HTT, TTT\}$$

Let's H_i be the event that the ith toss is a head. So for example:

$$H_1 = \{HHH, HHT, HTH, HTT\}$$

If we assign a probability of $\frac{1}{8}$ to each sample point, then using enumeration we see that $P(H_1) = P(H_2) = P(H_3) = \frac{1}{2}$.

Under this probability model, the events H_1, H_2, H_3 are mutually independent. To verify, we first write that:

$$P(H_1 \cap H_2 \cap H_3) = P(\{HHH\}) = \frac{1}{8} = \frac{1}{2} \cdot \frac{1}{2} \cdot \frac{1}{2} = P(H_1)P(H_2)P(H_3)$$

We must also check each pair. For example:

$$P(H_1 \cap H_2) = P(\{HHH, HHT\}) = \frac{2}{8} = \frac{1}{2} \cdot \frac{1}{2} = P(H_1)P(H_2)$$

The same applies to the two other pairs. Therefore H_1, H_2, H_3 are mutually independent. In general, we write that the probability of two independent events is the product of their probability: $P(A \cap B) = P(A).P(B)$. And we write that the probability of two disjoint independent events is the sum of their probability: $P(A \vee B) = P(A) + P(B)$.

If we consider a different outcome, we can define another probability distribution. For example, let's consider again the experiment in which a coin is tossed three times. This time we consider the random variable X as the number of heads obtained after three tosses.

A complete enumeration gives the same sample space as before:

$$S = \{HHH, HHT, HTH, THH, TTH, THT, HTT, TTT\}$$

But as we consider the number of heads, the random variable X will map the sample space to the following numbers this time:

s	HHH	HHT	HTH	THH	TTH	THT	HTT	TTT
X(s)	3	2	2	2	1	1	1	0

So the range for the random variable X is now $\{0,1,2,3\}$. If we assume the same probability for all points as before, that is $\frac{1}{8}$, then we can deduce the probability function on the range of X:

x	0	1	2	3
P(X=x)	$\frac{1}{8}$	$\frac{3}{8}$	$\frac{3}{8}$	$\frac{1}{8}$

Joint probability distributions

Let's come back to the first game: 2 heads and a 6 simultaneously, the hard game with a low probability of winning. We can associate to the coin toss experiment a random variable N, which is the number of heads after two tosses. This random variable summarizes our experiment very well and N can take the values 0, 1, or 2. So instead of saying we're interested in the event of having two heads, we can say equivalently that we are interested in the event $N=2$. This approach allows us to look at other events, such as having only one head (HT or TH) and even having zero heads (TT). We say that the function assigning a probability to each value of N is called a probability distribution. Another random variable is D, the number we obtain when we throw a dice.

When we consider the two experiments together (tossing a coin twice and throwing a dice), we are interested in the probability of obtaining either 0, 1, or 2 heads and at the same time obtaining either 1, 2, 3, 4, 5, or 6 with the dice. The probability distribution of these two random variables considered at the same time is written $P(N, D)$ and it is called a **joint probability distribution**.

If we keep adding more and more experiments and therefore more and more variables, we can write a very big and complex joint probability distribution. For example, I could be interested in the probability that it will rain tomorrow, that the stock market will rise and that there will be a traffic jam on the highway that I take to go to work. It's a complex one but not unrealistic. I'm almost sure that the stock market and the weather are really not dependent. However, the traffic condition and the weather are seriously connected. I would like to write the distribution *P(W, M, T)* — weather, market, traffic — but it seems to be overly complex. In fact, it is not and this is what we will see throughout this book.

A probabilistic graphical model is a joint probability distribution. And nothing else.

One last and very important notion regarding joint probability distributions is **marginalization**. When you have a probability distribution over several random variables, that is a joint probability distribution, you may want to *eliminate* some of the variables from this distribution to have a distribution on fewer variables. This operation is very important. The marginal distribution *p(X)* of a joint distribution *p(X, Y)* is obtained by the following operation:

$p(X) = \Sigma_y \ p(X,Y)$ where we sum the probabilities over all the possible values of *y*. By doing so, you can *eliminate* Y from *P(X, Y)*. As an exercise, I'll let you think about the link between this and the probability of two disjoint events that we saw earlier.

For the math-orientated readers, when *Y* is a continuous variable, the marginalization can be written as $p(X) = \int_y \ p(X,y)dy$.

This operation is extremely important and hard to compute for probabilistic graphical models and most if not all the algorithms for PGM try to propose an efficient solution to this problem. Thanks to these algorithms, we can do complex yet efficient models on many variables with real-world data.

Bayes' rule

Let's continue our exploration of the basic concepts we need to play with probabilistic graphical models. We saw the notion of marginalization, which is important because, when you have a complex model, you may want to extract information about one or a few variables of interest. And this is when marginalization is used.

But the two most important concepts are conditional probability and Bayes' rule.

A **conditional probability** is the probability of an event conditioned on the knowledge of another event. Obviously, the two events must be somehow dependent otherwise knowing one will not change anything for the other:

- What's the probability of rain tomorrow? And what's the probability of a traffic jam in the streets?

- Knowing it's going to rain tomorrow, what is now the probability of a traffic jam? Presumably higher than if you knew nothing.

This is a conditional probability. In more formal terms, we can write the following formula:

$$p(X|Y) = \frac{p(X,Y)}{p(Y)} \text{ and } P(Y|X) = \frac{P(X,Y)}{P(X)}$$

From these two equations we can easily deduce the Bayes formula:

$$P(X|Y) = \frac{P(Y|X).P(X)}{P(Y)}$$

(handwritten annotations: likelihood, prior, Posterior, normalization factor)

This formula is the most important and it helps invert probabilistic relationships. This is the *chef d'oeuvre* of Laplace's career and one of the most important formulas in modern science. Yet it is very simple.

In this formula, we call $P(X \mid Y)$ the posterior distribution of X given Y. Therefore, we also call $P(X)$ the prior distribution. We also call $P(Y \mid X)$ the likelihood and finally $P(Y)$ is the normalization factor.

The normalization factor needs a bit of explanation and development here. Recall that $P(X,Y) = P(Y|X)P(X)$. And also, we saw that $P(Y) = \Sigma_x \; P(X,Y)$, an operation we called marginalization, whose goal was to eliminate (or marginalize out) a variable from a joint probability distribution.

So from there, we can write $P(Y) = \Sigma_x \; P(X,Y) = \Sigma_x P(Y|X)P(X)$.

Thanks to this magic bit of simple algebra, we can rewrite the Bayes' formula in its general form and also the most convenient one:

$$P(X|Y) = \frac{P(Y|X).P(X)}{\Sigma_x P(Y|X)P(X)}$$

The simple beauty of this form is that we only need to specify and use $P(Y | X)$ and $P(X)$, that is, the prior and likelihood. Despite the simple form, the sum in the denominator, as we will see in the rest of this book, can be a hard problem to solve and advanced techniques will be required for advanced problems.

Interpreting the Bayes' formula

Now that we saw the famous formula with X and Y, two random variables, let me rewrite it with two other variables. After all, the letters are not important but it can shed some light on the intuition behind this formula:

$$P(\theta | D) = \frac{p(D|\theta).P(\theta)}{\sum_{\theta_i} P(D|\theta)P(\theta)}$$

The intuition behind these concepts is the following:

- The **prior distribution** $P(\theta)$ is what I believe about X before everything else is known—my initial belief.
- The **likelihood** given a value for θ, what is the data D that I could *generate*, or in other terms what is the probability of D for all values of θ?
- The **posterior distribution** $P(\theta | D)$ is finally the new belief I have about θ given some data D I observed.

This formula also gives the basis of a forward process to update my beliefs about the variable θ. Applying Bayes' rule will calculate the new distribution of θ. And if I receive new information again, I can update my beliefs again, and again.

A first example of Bayes' rule

In this section we will look at our first Bayesian program in R. We will define **discrete random variables**, that is, random variables that can only take a predefined number of values. Let's say we have a machine that makes light bulbs. You want to know if the machine works as planned or if it's broken. In order to do that you can test each bulb but that would be too many bulbs to test. With only a few samples and Bayes' rule you can estimate if the machine is correctly working or not.

When building a Bayesian model, we need to always set up the two main components:

- The prior distribution
- The likelihood

In this example, we won't need a specific package; we just need to write a simple function to implement a simple form of the Bayes' rule.

The prior distribution is our initial belief on how the machine is working or not. We identified a first random variable M for the state of the machine. This random variable can have two states *{working, broken}*. We believe our machine is working well because it's a good machine, so let's say the prior distribution is as follows:

$$P(M = working) = 0.99$$
$$P(M = broken) = 0.01$$

It simply says that our belief that the machine is working is really high, with a probability of 99% and only a 1% chance that it is broken. Here, clearly we're using the Bayesian interpretation of probability because we don't have many machines but just one. We could also ask the machine's vendor about the frequency of working machines he or she is able to produce. And we could use his or her number and, in that case, this probability would have a frequentist interpretation. Nevertheless, the Bayes' rule works in all the cases.

The second random variable is L and it is the light bulb produced by the machine. The light bulb can either be *good* or *bad*. So this random variable will have two states again *{good, bad}*.

Again, we need to give a prior distribution for the light bulb variable L: in the Bayes' formula, it is required that we specify a prior distribution and the likelihood distribution. In this case, the likelihood is $P(L \mid M)$ and not simply $P(L)$.

Here we need in fact to define two probability distributions: one when the machine works $M = working$ and one when the machine is broken $M = broken$. And we ask the question twice:

- How likely is it to have a good or a bad light bulb when the machine is working?
- How likely is it to have a good or a bad light bulb when the machine is not working?

Let's try to give our best guess, either Bayesian or frequentist, because we have some statistics:

$$P(L = good \mid M = working) = 0.99$$
$$P(L = bad \mid M = working) = 0.01$$
$$P(L = good \mid M = broken) = 0.6$$
$$P(L = bad \mid M = broken) = 0.4$$

Here we believe that, if the machine is working, it will only give one bad light bulb out of 100, which is even higher than what we said before. But in this case, we know that the machine is working so we expect a very high success rate. However, if the machine is broken, we say we expect at least 40% of the light bulbs to be bad. From now on, we have fully specified our model and we can start using it.

Using a Bayesian model is to compute posterior distributions when a new fact is available. In our case, we want to know if the machine is working knowing that we just observed that our latest light bulb was not working. So we want to compute P(M | L). We just specified P(M) and P(L | M), so the last thing we have to do is to use the Bayes' formula to invert the probability distribution.

For example, let's say the last produced light bulb is bad, that is, L = bad. Using the Bayes formula we obtain:

$$P\big(M = working \mid L = bad\big) =$$

$$\frac{P\big(L = bad \mid M = working\big).P\big(M = working\big)}{P\big(L = bad \mid M = working\big)P\big(M = working\big) + P\big(L = bad \mid M = broken\big)P\big(M = working\big)}$$

$$= $$

$$\frac{0.01 \times 0.99}{0.01 \times 0.99 + 0.4 \times 0.01} = 0.71$$

Or if you prefer, a 71% chance that the machine is working. It's lower but follows our intuition that the machine might still work. After all even if we received a bad light bulb, it's only one and maybe the next will still be good.

Let's try to redo the same problem, with equal priors on the state of the machine: a 50% chance the machine is working and 50% the machine is broken. The result is therefore:

$$\frac{0.01 \times 0.5}{0.01 \times 0.5 + 0.4 \times 0.5} = 0.024$$

It is a 2.4% chance the machine is working! That's very low. Indeed, given the apparent quality of this machine, as modeled in the likelihood, it appears very surprising that the machine can produce a bad light bulb. In this case, we didn't make the assumption that the machine was working as in the previous example, and having a bad light bulb can be seen as an indication that something is wrong.

A first example of Bayes' rule in R

After seeing this previous example, the first legitimate question one can ask is what we would do if we observed more than one light bulb. Indeed, it seems a bit strange to conclude that the machine needs to be repaired only after seeing one bad light bulb. The Bayesian way to do it is to use the posterior as the new prior and update the posterior distribution in sequence. As it would be a bit onerous to do that by hand, we will write our first Bayesian program in R.

The following code is a function that computes the posterior distribution of a random variable given the prior distribution and the likelihood and a sequence of observed data. This function takes three arguments: the prior distribution, the likelihood, and a sequence of data. The prior and data are a vector and the likelihood a matrix:

```
prior <- c(working = 0.99, broken = 0.01)

likelihood <- rbind(
    working = c(good=0.99, bad=0.01), broken = c(good=0.6,
    bad=0.4))

data <- c("bad","bad","bad","bad")
```

So we defined three variables, the prior with two states working and broken, the likelihood we specified for each condition of the machine (working or broken), and the distribution over the variable L of the light bulb. So that's four values in total and the R matrix is indeed like the conditional distribution we defined in the previous section:

```
likelihood

          good     bad

working   0.99     0.01

broken    0.60     0.40
```

The data variable contains the sequence of observed light bulbs we will use to test our machine and compute the posterior probabilities. So, now we can define our Bayesian update function as follows:

```
bayes <- function(prior, likelihood, data)
{
  posterior <- matrix(0, nrow=length(data), ncol=length(prior))
  dimnames(posterior) <- list(data, names(prior))

  initial_prior <- prior
  for(i in 1:length(data))
  {
    posterior[i, ] <-
      prior*likelihood[ , data[i]]/
```

```
      sum(prior * likelihood[ , data[i]])

   prior <- posterior[i , ]
 }

  return(rbind(initial_prior,posterior))
}
```

This function does the following:

- It creates a matrix to store the results of the successive computation of the posterior distributions
- Then for each data it computes the posterior distribution given the current prior: you can see the Bayes formula in the R code, exactly as we saw it earlier
- Finally, the new prior is the current posterior and the same process can be re-iterated

In the end, the function returns a matrix with the initial prior and all subsequent posterior distributions.

Let's do a few runs to understand how it works. We will use the function `matplot` to draw the evolution of the two distributions, one for the posterior probability that the machine is working (in green) and the other in red, meaning that the machine is broken:

```
matplot( bayes(prior,likelihood,data), t='b', lty=1, pch=20,
col=c(3,2))
```

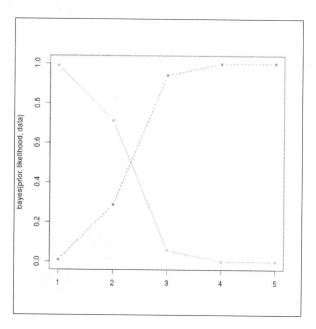

The result can be seen on the following graph: as the bad light bulbs arrive, the probability that the machine will fail quickly falls (the plain or green line). We expected something like 1 bad light bulb out of 100, and not that many. So this machine needs maintenance now. The red or dashed line represents the probability that the machine is broken.

If the prior was different, we would have seen a different evolution. For example, let's say that we have no idea if the machine is broken or not, that is, we give an equal chance to each situation:

```
prior <- c(working = 0.5, broken = 0.5)
```

Run the code again:

```
matplot( bayes(prior,likelihood,data), t='b', lty=1, pch=20,
col=c(3,2))
```

Again we obtain a quick convergence to very high probabilities that the machine is broken, which is not surprising given the long sequence of bad light bulbs:

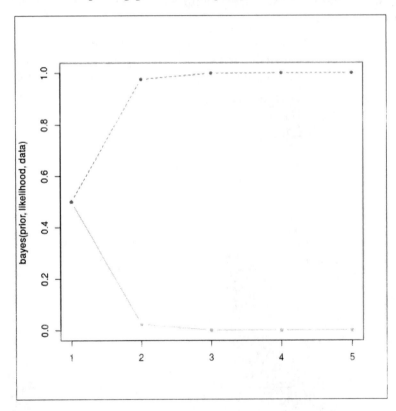

If we keep playing with the data we might see different behaviors again. For example, let's say we assume the machine is working well, with a 99% probability. And we observe a sequence of 10 light bulbs, among which the first one is bad. In R we have:

```
prior=c(working=0.99,broken=0.01)
data=c("bad","good","good","good","good","good","good","good","good","go
od")
matplot(bayes(prior,likelihood,data),t='b',pch=20,col=c(3,2))
```

And the result is given in the following graph:

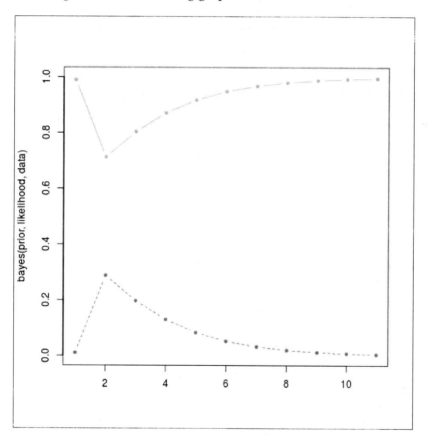

The algorithm hesitates at first because, given such a good machine, it's unlikely to see a bad light bulb, but then it will converge back to high probabilities again, because the sequence of good light bulbs does not indicate any problem.

This concludes our first example of a Bayesian model with R. In the rest of this chapter, we will see how to create real-world models, with more than just two very simple random variables, and how to solve two important problems:

- The problem of inference, which is the problem of computing the posterior distribution when we receive new data
- The problem of learning, which is the determination of prior probabilities from a dataset

A careful reader should now ask: doesn't this little algorithm we just saw solve the problem of inference? Indeed it does, but only when one has two discrete variables, which is a bit too simple to capture the complexity of the world. We will introduce now the core of this book and the main tool for performing Bayesian inference: probabilistic graphical models.

Probabilistic graphical models

In the last section of this chapter, we introduce probabilistic graphical models as a generic framework to build and use complex probabilistic models from simple building blocks. Such complex models are often necessary to represent the complexity of the task to solve. Complex doesn't mean complicated and often the simple things are the best and most efficient. Complex means that, in order to represent and solve tasks where we have a lot of inputs, components, or data, we need a model that is not completely trivial but reaches the necessary degree of complexity.

Such complex problems can be decomposed into simpler problems that will interact with each other. Ultimately, the most simple building block will be one variable. This variable will have a random value, or a value subject to uncertainty as we saw in the previous section.

Probabilistic models

If you remember, we saw that it is possible to represent really advanced concepts using a probability distribution; when we have many random variables, we call this distribution a joint distribution. Sometimes it is not impossible to have hundreds if not thousands or more of those random variables. Representing such a big distribution is extremely hard and in most cases impossible.

For example, in medical diagnoses, each random variable could represent a symptom. We can have dozens of them. Other random variables could represent the age of the patient, the gender of the patient, his or her temperature, blood pressure, and so on. We can use many different variables to represent the health state of a patient. We can also add other information such as recent weather conditions, the age of the patient, and his or her diet.

Then there are two tasks we want to solve with such a complex system:

- From a database of patients, we want to assess and discover all the probability distributions and their associated parameters, automatically of course.

- We want to put questions to the model, such as, "If I observe a series of symptoms, is my patient healthy or not?" Similarly, "If I change this or that in my patient's diet and give this drug, will my patient recover?"

However, there is something important: in such a model we would like to use another important piece of knowledge, maybe one of the most important: interactions between the various components—in other words, dependencies between the random variables. For example, there are obvious dependencies between symptoms and disease. On the other end, diet and symptoms can have a more distant dependency or can be dependent through another variable such as age or gender.

Finally, all the reasoning that is done with such a model is probabilistic in nature. From the observation of a variable X, we want to infer the posterior distribution of some other variables and have their probability rather than a simple *yes* or *no* answer. Having a probability gives us a richer answer than a binary response.

Graphs and conditional independence

Let's make a simple computation. Imagine we have two binary random variables such as the one we saw in the previous section of this chapter. Let's call them X and Y. The joint probability distribution over these two variables is $P(X,Y)$. They are binary so they can take two values each, which we will call x_1, x_2 and y_1, y_2, for the sake of clarity.

How many probability values do we need to specify? Four in total for $P(X=x_1, Y=y_1)$, $P(X=x_1, Y=y_2)$, $P(X=x_2, Y=y_1)$, and $P(X=x_2, Y=y_2)$.

Let's say we have now not two binary random variables, but ten. It's still a very simple model, isn't it? Let's call the variables $X_1, X_2, X_3, X_4, X_5, X_6, X_7, X_8, X_9, X_{10}$. In this case, we need to provide $2^{10} = 1024$ values to determine our joint probability distribution. And what if we add another 10 variables for a total of 20 variables? It's still a very small model. But we need to specify $2^{20} = 1048576$ values. This is more than a million values. So for such a simple model, the task becomes simply impossible!

Probabilistic graphical models is the right framework to describe such models in a compact way and allow their construction and use in a most efficient manner. In fact, it is not unheard of to use probabilistic graphical models with thousands of variables. Of course, the computer model doesn't store billions of values, but in fact uses conditional independence in order to make the model tractable and representable in a computer's memory. Moreover, conditional independence adds structural knowledge to the model, which can make a massive difference.

In a probabilistic graphical model, such knowledge between variables can be represented with a graph. Here is an example from the medical world: how to diagnose a cold. This is just an example and by no means medical advice. It is over-simplified for the sake of simplicity. We have several random variables such as:

- *Se*: The season of the year
- *N*: The nose is blocked
- *H*: The patient has a headache
- *S*: The patient regularly sneezes
- *C*: The patient coughs
- *Cold*: The patient has a cold

Because each of the symptoms can exist in different degrees, it is natural to represent the variables as random variables. For example, if the patient's nose is a bit blocked, we will assign a probability of, say, 60% to this variable, that is $P(N=blocked)=0.6$ and $P(N=not\ blocked)=0.4$.

In this example, the probability distribution $P(Se,N,H,S,C,Cold)$ will require $4 * 2^5 = 128$ values in total (4 seasons and 2 values for each other random variables). It's quite a lot and honestly it's quite hard to determine things such as the probability that the nose is not blocked and that the patient has a headache and sneezes and so on.

However, we can say that a headache is not directly related to a cough or a blocked nose, except when the patient has a cold. Indeed, the patient could have a headache for many other reasons.

Moreover, we can say that the **Season** has quite a direct effect on **Sneezing, Blocked Nose**, or **Cough** but less or none on **Headache**. In a probabilistic graphical model, we will represent these dependency relationships with a graph, as follows, where each random variable is a node in the graph and each relationship is an arrow between two nodes:

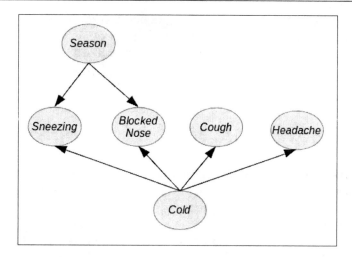

As you can see in the preceding figure, there is a direct relationship between each node and each variable of the probabilistic graphical model and also a direct relationship between arrows and the way we can simplify the joint probability distribution in order to make it tractable.

Using a graph as a model to simplify a complex (and sometimes complicated) distribution presents numerous benefits:

- First of all, as we observed in the previous example, and in general when we model a problem, random variables interact directly with only small subsets of other random variables. Therefore, this promotes a more compact and tractable model.

- Knowledge and dependencies represented in a graph are easy to understand and communicate.

- The graph induces a compact representation of the joint probability distribution and is easy to make computations with.

- Algorithms to perform inference and learning can use graph theory and the associated algorithms to improve and facilitate all the inference and learning algorithms: compared to the raw joint probability distribution, using a PGM will speed up computations by several orders of magnitude.

Factorizing a distribution

In the previous example on the diagnosis of the common cold, we defined a simple model with a few variables *Se, N, H, S, C,* and *R*. We saw that, for such a simple expert system, we needed 128 parameters!

We also saw that we can make a few independence assumptions based only on common sense or common knowledge. Later in this book, we will see how to discover those assumptions from a data set (also called **structural learning**).

So we can rewrite our joint probability distribution taking into account these assumptions as follows:

$$P(Se, N, H, S, C, Cold) = P(Se)P(S \mid Se, Cold)P(N \mid Se, Cold)P(Cold)P(C \mid Cold)P(H \mid Cold)$$

In this distribution, we did a factorization; that is, we expressed the original joint distribution as a product of factors. In this case, the factors are simpler probability distributions such as *P(C | Cold)*, the probability of coughing given that one has a cold. And as we considered all the variables to be binary (except *Season*, which can take of course four values), each small factor (distribution) will need only a few parameters to be determined: $4 + 2^3 + 2^3 + 2 + 2^2 + 2^2 = 30$. Only 30 easy parameters instead of 128! It's a massive improvement.

I said the parameters are easy, because they're easy to determine, either by hand or from data. For example, we don't know if the patient has a cold or not, so we can assign equal probability to the variable *Cold*, that is *P(Cold = true)=P(Cold = false)=0.5*.

Similarly, it's easy to determine *P(C | Cold)* because, if the patient has a cold *(Cold=true)*, he or she will likely cough. If he or she has no cold, then chances will be low for the patient to cough, but not zero because the cause could be something else.

Directed models

In general, a directed probabilistic graphical model factorizes a joint distribution over the random variables $X_1, X_2...X_n$ as follows:

$$P(X_1, X_2, \ldots, X_n) = \prod_{i=1}^{N} P(X_i \mid pa(X_i))$$

pa(X$_i$) is the subset of parent variables of the variable X_i as defined in the graph.

The parents are easy to read on a graph: when an arrow goes from **A** to **B**, then **A** is the parent of **B**. A node can have as many children as needed and a node can have as many parents as needed too.

Directed models are good for representing problems in which *causality* has to be modeled. It is also a good model for learning from parameters because each local probability distribution is easy to learn.

Several times in this chapter, we mentioned the fact that PGM can be built using simple blocks and assembled to make a bigger model. In the case of directed models, the blocks are the small probability distributions $P(X_i \mid pa(X_i))$.

Moreover, if one wants to extend the model by defining new variables and relations, it is as simple as extending the graph. The algorithms designed for directed PGM work for any graph, whatever its size.

Nevertheless, not all probability distributions can be represented by a directed PGM and sometimes it is necessary to relax certain assumptions.

Also it is important to note the graph must be *acyclic*. It means that you can't have an arrow from node **A** to node **B** and from node **B** to node **A** as in the following figure:

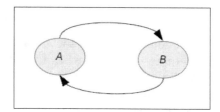

In fact, this graph does not represent a factorization at all as defined earlier and it would mean something like *A is a cause of B while at the same time B is a cause of A*. It's paradoxical and has no equivalent mathematical formula.

When the assumption or relationships are not directed, there exists a second form of probabilistic graphical model in which all the edges are undirected. It is called an undirected probabilistic graphical model or a Markov network.

Undirected models

An undirected probabilistic graphical model factorizes a joint distribution over the random variables $X_1, X_2 \ldots X_n$ as follows:

$$P(X_1, X_2, \ldots, X_n) = \frac{1}{Z} \prod_{c=1}^{C} \varphi_c(\chi_c)$$

This formula needs a bit of explanation:

- The first term on the left-hand side is our now usual joint probability distribution

- The constant Z is a normalization constant, ensuring that the right-hand term will sum to 1, because it's a probability distribution

- φ_c is a factor over a subset of variables χ_c such that each member of this subset is a maximal clique, that is a sub-graph in which all the nodes are connected together:

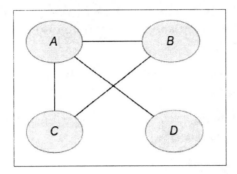

In the preceding figure, we have four nodes and the φ_c functions will be defined on the subsets that are maximal cliques — that is {ABC} and {A,D}. So the distribution is not very complex after all. This type of model is used a lot in applications such as computer vision, image processing, finance, and many more applications where the relationships between the variables follow a regular pattern.

Examples and applications

It's about time to talk about the applications of probabilistic graphical models. There are so many applications that I would need another hundred pages to describe a subset of them. As we saw, it is a very powerful framework to model complex probabilistic models by making them easy to interpret and tractable.

In this section, we will use our two previous models: the light bulb machine and the cold diagnosis.

We recall that the cold diagnosis model has the following factorization:

$$P(Se,N,H,S,C,Cold) = P(Se)P(S\,|\,Se,Cold)P(N\,|\,Se,Cold)P(Cold)P(C\,|\,Cold)P(H\,|\,Cold)$$

The light bulb machine, though, is defined by two variables only: L and M. And the factorization is very simple:

$$P(L,M) = P(M).P(L\,|\,M)$$

The graph corresponding to this distribution is simply:

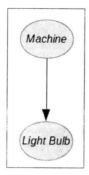

In order to represent our probabilistic graphical model, we will use an R package called gRain. To install it:

```
source("http://bioconductor.org/biocLite.R")
biocLite()
install.packages("gRain")
```

Note that the installation can take several minutes because this package depends on many other packages (and especially one we will use often called gRbase) and provides the base functions for manipulating graphs.

When the package is installed, you can load the base package with:

```
library("gRbase")
```

First of all, we want to define a simple undirected graph with five variables A, B, C, D and E:

```
graph <- ug("A:B:E + C:E:D")
class(graph)
```

$$ug(\sim A:B:E + C:E:D)$$

We define a graph with a clique between A, B, and E, and another clique between C, E, and D. This will form a butterfly graph. The syntax is very simple: in the string each clique is separated by a + and each clique is defined by the name of each variable separated by a colon.

Next we need to install a graph visualization library. We will use the popular Rgraphviz and to install it you can enter:

```
install.packages("Rgraphviz")
plot(graph)
```

You will obtain your first undirected graph as follows:

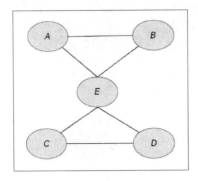

Next we want to define a directed graph. Let's say we have again the same *{A,B,C,D,E}* variables:

```
dag <- dag("A + B:A + C:B + D:B + E:C:D")
dag
plot(dag)
```

The syntax is again very simple: a node without parent comes alone such as A; otherwise parents are specified by the list of nodes separated by colons.

In this library, several syntaxes are available to define graphs, and you can also build them node by node. Throughout the book we will use several notations as well as a very important representation: the matrix notation. Indeed, a graph can be equivalently represented by a squared matrix where each row and each column represents a node and the coefficient in the matrix will be 1 is there is an edge; 0 otherwise. If the graph is undirected, the matrix will be symmetric; otherwise, the matrix can be anything.

Finally, with this second test we obtain the following graph:

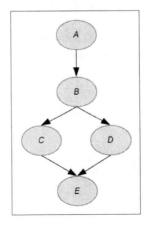

Now we want to define a simple graph for the light bulb machine and provide numerical probabilities. Then we will do our computations again and check that the results are the same.

First we define the values for each node:

```
machine_val <- c("working","broken")
light_bulb_val <- c("good","bad")
```

Then we define the numerical values as percentages for the two random variables:

```
machine_prob <- c(99,1)
light_bulb_prob <- c(99,1,60,40)
```

The next step is to define the random variables with gRain:

```
M <- cptable(~machine, values=machine_prob, levels=machine_val)
L <- cptable(~light_bulb|machine, values=light_bulb_prob, levels=light_
bulb_val)
```

Here, cptable means conditional probability table: it's a term to designate the memory representation of a probability distribution in the case of a discrete random variable. We will come back to this notion in *Chapter 2, Exact Inference*.

Finally, we can compile the new graphical model before using it. Again, this notion will make more sense in *Chapter 2, Exact Inference*. when we look at inference algorithms such as the **Junction Tree Algorithm**:

```
plist <- compileCPT(list(M,L))
plist
```

When printing the network, the result should be as follows:

```
CPTspec with probabilities:
 P( machine )
 P( light_bulb | machine )
```

Here, you clearly recognize the probability distributions that we defined earlier in this chapter.

If we print the variables' distribution we will find again what we had before:

```
plist$machine
plist$light_bulb
```

This will output the following result:

```
> plist$machine
machine
working   broken
   0.99     0.01
> plist$light_bulb
            machine
light_bulb working broken
      good    0.99    0.6
       bad    0.01    0.4
```

And now we ask the model the posterior probability. The first step is to enter an evidence into the model (that is to say that we observed a bad light bulb) by doing as follows:

```
net <- grain(plist)
net2 <- setEvidence(net, evidence=list(light_bulb="bad"))
querygrain(net2, nodes=c("machine"))
```

The library will compute the result by applying its inference algorithm and will output the following result:

```
$machine
machine
  working      broken
0.7122302  0.2877698
```

And this result is rigorously the same as we obtained with the Bayes method we defined earlier.

Therefore we are now ready to create more powerful models and explore the different algorithms suitable for solving different problems. This is what we're going to learn in the next chapter on exact inference in graphical models.

Summary

In this first chapter we learned the base concepts of probabilities

We saw how and why they are used to represent uncertainty about data and knowledge, while also introducing the Bayes formula. This is the most important formula to compute posterior probabilities — that is, to update our beliefs and knowledge about a fact when new data is available

We saw what a joint probability distribution is and learnt that they can quickly become too complex and intractable to deal with. We learned the basics of probabilistic graphical models as a generic framework to perform tractable, efficient, and easy modeling with probabilistic models. Finally, we introduced the different types of probabilistic graphical model and learned how to use R packages to write our first models

In the next chapter, we will learn the first set of algorithms to do Bayesian inference with probabilistic graphical models — that is, to put questions and queries to our models. We will introduce new features of the R packages and, at the same time, we'll learn how these algorithms work and can be used in an efficient manner.

2
Exact Inference

After building a graphical model, one of the main tasks one wants to perform is putting questions and queries to the model. There are many ways to use graphical models and the representation they give from a joint probability distribution. For example, we can study interactions between random variables. We can also see if any correlation or causality is captured by the model. Moreover, as probability models governing the random variables are parameterized, it means that their probability distribution is fully known through being familiar with some numerical parameters. We might be interested in knowing the values of those parameters when other variables are observed.

The main focus of this chapter is on introducing algorithms to query a distribution that uses the model and observations on a subset of variables in order to discover the posterior probability distribution on another subset. It is not necessary to observe and query all the variables. In fact, all the algorithms we are going to see in this chapter can be performed on any observed subset and any queried subset.

There are mainly two types of queries:

- **Probabilistic queries**, in which we observe a subset E of variables and choose an instantiation e of these variables, which we call evidence, and then we compute the posterior distribution of a subset Y of the set X of variables: $P(Y \mid E = e)$.

- **MAP queries**; These refer to finding a join assignment to a subset of variables having the highest probability. Again, if we call E the set of observed variables and Z the remaining variables of the model, then the MAP assignment is defined by $MAP(Z \mid E = e) = argmax_z P(z, e)$. In other words, we seek for the values of the non-observed variables that would have the highest probability if we observed the assignment $E=e$.

The aim of this chapter is to introduce the main algorithms for solving the problem of inference exactly; that is, the problem of answering such queries. In general, the problem of inference boils down to finding a posterior distribution by applying the Bayes rule. In mathematical terms, if we call X the set of all the variables of the model, E the set of observed variables (evidence), and Z the set of hidden variables, or non-observed variables, then computing an inference on a graphical model finds:

$$P(Z \mid E, \theta) = \frac{P(Z, E \mid \theta)}{P(E \mid \theta)} = \frac{P(Z, E \mid \theta)}{\sum_{z \in Z} P(Z = z, E \mid \theta)}$$

For example, in a medical problem, we want to know all possible diseases given a set of observed symptoms. In a speech recognition system, we want to know the most likely sequence of words that generated the sound that has been recorded (that is, the voice of the speaker). In a radar tracking system, we want to know the probability distribution of the location of the tracked object given readings from radar. In a recommendation system, we want to know the posterior distributions on the products to sell, given the latest clicks of a user on a merchant website, and therefore we rank and suggest the best five products to the customer.

All these problems, and many more, always require the computation of a posterior distribution. In order to solve this complex problem, we are going to see a different type of algorithm, which will use the structure of the underlying graph in the probabilistic graphical model, to perform efficient computations. However, in the first part of the chapter, in order to understand how it works, we will see how to perform a naive computation, which is not very efficient but serves as a framework from which to improve efficiency. It is called variable elimination and it simply eliminates each variable, step by step, that is not required in the query.

Next we will see that it is possible to reuse previous computations and improve the efficiency of the algorithm with a second algorithm called the Sum-Product algorithm. We will apply this to different types of probabilistic graphical model, and in particular to a graph with a hierarchy called trees. This will serve as an introduction to the last and most important algorithm, the junction tree algorithm, which takes any graph and transforms it into a tree to produce an efficient schedule of computations. This algorithm is implemented in most of the R packages that we're going to use throughout this chapter.

In this chapter you will learn how to perform simple inference, improve the efficiency of the computations, and finally work with graphical models that are as complex as you need to capture the essence of real-world problems. We will introduce algorithms written in R and functions from R packages, such as `gRain`, `gR`, and `rHugin`.

But before we start with all the mathematics and programming, the first section will focus on the design of Probabilistic Graphical Models and will introduce examples of expert systems; it will also show how to represent legacy models as graphical models and benefit from this powerful tool.

The chapter will therefore be organized as follows:

- Building graphical models
- Variable elimination
- Sum-product and belief updates
- The junction tree algorithm

Building graphical models

The design of a graphical model usually takes into consideration two different aspects. First of all, we need to identify the variables involved in the model. The variables can refer to facts we can observe or measure, such as a temperature, a price, a distance, a number of items, an interval of time, or any other value. A variable can also represent a simple fact that can be true or false.

At the same time, and this is why we're building such models, the variables can capture parts of the problem that we cannot directly measure or estimate but that are related to the problem. For example, a physician is able to see and measure a set of symptoms for a patient. However diseases are not facts that can be directly observed. They can only be deduced from the observation of several symptoms. Let's take the common cold. It is natural to say that someone has a cold, and in practice everybody understands what it means. However, there is no such thing such as a cold, but rather one has a viral infection located in the upper respiratory tract (the nose) where the infection is a proliferation of a certain type of rhinovirus. It's rather complex, but it is the common cold.

Directly inferring that someone has a cold is almost impossible unless one samples mucus and estimates that the quantity of rhinoviruses present in the sample is enough to say the patient has this specific disease. Another method is to infer from simple symptoms such as a headache and running nose that the patient is affected. In this case, the variable representing the fact the patient has a cold is not directly observable.

The second aspect is the graph, which in fact represents the dependencies between the variable, how they are related to each other, how they can interact, directly or indirectly. If you learned about statistics before, you probably used the notion of correlation. In the case of a graphical model, the dependency between two variables is understood in a larger sense. Indeed, correlation only denotes a linear relationship between variables.

For example, a variable representing a symptom and a variable representing a disease can be connected because there is a direct relationship between these two variables.

Types of random variable

In most cases, the variables we will be using are discrete variables. The reason for that is because we are interested in modeling facts that can be true or false, or that can take a specific number of values. Another reason is because it is very common to make models with discrete variables in many scientific fields and finally because the math behind discrete variable graphical models is easier to understand and implement.

A discrete random variable X is defined over a finite sample space $S = \{v_1, v_2 ... v_n\}$. Examples of discrete random variables are:

- A dice D has samples over the set of numbers $\{1, 2, 3, 4, 5, 6\}$
- A coin C is defined over the set $\{T, H\}$
- A symptom S is defined over the value $\{true, false\}$
- A letter in a word is defined over the bigger set $\{a, b, c, d, e, ..., z\}$
- A word is defined over a very large set of English words $\{the, at, in, bread, ..., computer, ...\}$: the set is however finite
- A size can be defined over a finite set of numbers, say $\{0, 1, 2, 3, ..., 1000\}$

A continuous random variable is defined on a continuous sample space such as $\mathbb{R}$, $\mathbb{C}$, or any other interval. It is of course possible to define random variables on a multi-dimensional set such as $\mathbb{R}^n$ but, depending on the meaning associated to each dimension, it is sometimes interesting to split each dimension into n distinct random variables, each defined on $\mathbb{R}$. Examples of continuous random variables are:

- A distance in kilometers
- A temperature
- A price
- The mean of another random variable
- The variance of another random variable

The last two examples are very important when one considers a Bayesian treatment of a problem and can lead to powerful representation of a machine learning problem. Indeed, in a Bayesian approach, all quantities are considered as random variables. Therefore, if we define a random variable following a Gaussian distribution $N(\mu, \sigma^2)$, we can go further and consider μ and σ^2 to be random variables too.

And in fact, in a graphical model, it is often useful to consider many parameters as random variables and connect these parameters together in the graph. The connection can also be based on common-sense relationships, causal interactions, or any dependency that is strong enough to exist between two variables.

Building graphs

There are many reasons to connect variables in a graph and, as we will see later in this chapter, there are also many algorithms to automatically learn such connections from a dataset. If you read the scientific literature, you will certainly find references to causality, sparse models, or factorization. All of these reasons are good enough to connect two variables in a graphical model. In this section we will build such models and see what happen when two variables are connected, in terms of both the model and flow of information, with an important notion called **d-separation**.

Another important aspect of making graphical models is modularization. This is one of the most attractive aspects of graphical models, because you can build complex models from simpler blocks and extend known models by simply extending their graph.

Then learning the parameters and querying the model boil down to the application of the same learning and inference algorithms.

Let's see now a few practical and theoretical examples of graphs and the type of problem they capture.

Probabilistic expert system

Let's say we want to perform the medical diagnosis of tuberculosis. Before diving into this example, a word of caution for the reader: the author of this book has no medical skills and knowledge. He specializes in the field and topic of this book and machine learning. Therefore, the following example's only purpose is to show how to build a simple graphical model and must not be used for medical purposes. Moreover, the following example is based on: http://en.wikipedia.org/wiki/Tuberculosis_diagnosis.

Tuberculosis is caused by a bacteria called Mycobacterium tuberculosis. Only a clinical examination with a biological analysis can detect the bacteria and confirm the disease or not. However, a physical examination can reveal clues about tuberculosis and lead the physician to decide that a thorough clinical examination is needed to confirm or not the presence of the bacteria in the patient's body. Moreover, a complete medical evaluation for tuberculosis must include the medical history, a physical examination, a chest X-ray, and a microbiological examination. So, if we look at the possible symptoms and examinations, we can also identify corresponding random variables that will be part of our model:

- C: This is prolonged cough for more than three weeks. C can be true or false.

- P: This is chest pain. It can be true or false.

- H: This is hemoptysis. Again we have a binary variable with true or false values and N for night sweats, which is a binary variable too.

- L: This is appetite loss. This is more subjective and we can grade it with three values: *{low, medium, strong}* to denote the intensity of the appetite loss.

- Finally, as we said, only a microbiological study can confirm tuberculosis, while other symptoms can only presume it. So we need two random variables, one binary called M for the microbiological study that says whether the bacteria has been found or not and one that decides if the patient has confirmed, probable, presumed, or negative tuberculosis. It's a random variable with four states.

In order to make our graphical model, we need now to perform two things: first of all we need a graph to connect our random variables and then we need to estimate prior probabilities associated with each variable — or, if you prefer, with each node in the graph. For the second task, estimating probabilities requires an expert medical knowledge that is clearly beyond the scope of this book (and beyond the skills of the author as stated before). So we will simply give names to the probabilities, such as x^1, x^2, x^3, and so on.

A symptom is in general caused by the presence of a disease and not the other way around. For example, night sweats are not the cause of tuberculosis; it's clearly the other way around. Moreover night sweats could be caused by many other things, such as a powerful heater in the bedroom. However, the presence of the bacteria causes the disease. In fact, if a bacteria is present but in a very small quantity, it could not cause the disease. This simple reasoning gives us a way to design our graph.

Let's start with the binary symptoms C, P, H, and N. They are caused by the disease T. The variable L can be added following the same principle too and therefore the graph should be as follows:

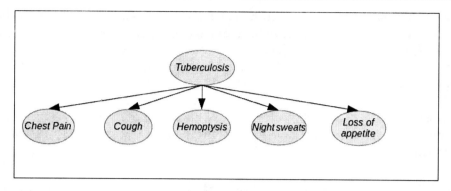

We see there is a pattern in the way variables are connected together. This pattern is very common when one deals with causes and consequences in a graphical model. If we apply the same idea to the relationships between the microbiological study M and the disease T, we will have the following interaction:

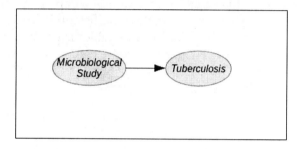

So the final graph when we join the two previous graphs together is the following:

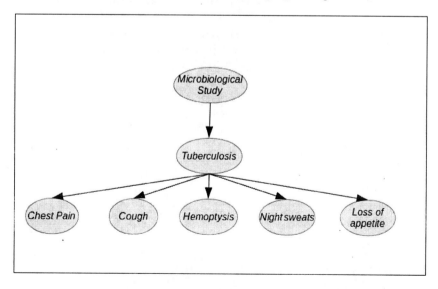

And what we just did is a very important aspect of graphical models: we joined two sub-models together in order to form one that is more advanced and captures what we need more effectively. In fact, we could add more symptoms and diseases in the same graph so that we would be able to differentiate between, for example, tuberculosis and pneumonia or any other disease that could have similar symptoms. By computing the posterior probability of each disease given a few symptoms, the physician could decide which treatment is the most appropriate for the most likely disease. This form of probabilistic graphical model is sometimes called a **probabilistic expert system**.

Basic structures in probabilistic graphical models

We continue our exploration of structures and patterns in graphical models by looking at different types of structure we can have and their properties. We will conclude this part by implementing and displaying some of them in R using various packages.

If we have many causes for the same fact, the causes will point to the fact in the graph. This structure is very common and very inefficient! It should be avoided at all times except in cases where the number of variables is not big. Indeed, let's say we have causes C_1 to C_n, which are binary variables, and a fact F, which is a binary variable too. As we saw in the first chapter, the (local) probability distribution associated to this will be: $P(F \mid C_1, C_2 \ldots C_n)$.

Knowing that all the variables are binary, we will need to represent a table with $2n+1$ values. If $n=10$, which is not big in fact, we will need 2,048 values! That's a lot of probabilities to find. But if we have 31 causes, $2^{31+1} = 2^{32} = 4,294,967,296$!!!

Yes, you need more than 4 billion values, just for representing 31 causes and a fact. With standard double floating point values, that totals 34,359,738,368 bytes in your computer's memory, that is, 32 GB! For such a small model, it's a bit too much. If your variables don't have two but, say, k values instead, you will need k^{n+1} values, to represent the previous conditional probability. That's a lot!

The following graph shows the causes:

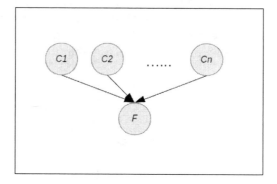

We can reason further about the causes, as some of them might not be directly related to the fact but instead might be causing other causes. In that case, we can give a hierarchy of causes in the graph as follows:

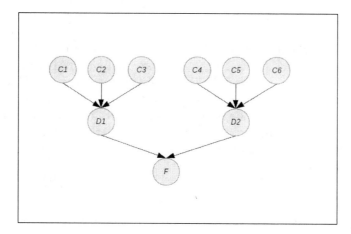

In this example, we deal with eight causes, but each local probability distribution, such as for example $P(D_1 \mid C_1, C_2, C_3)$ only involves four variables at most. This is tractable.

When we look at sequences of variables, another structure comes to mind, in which we don't capture causality but rather a sequence of variables in time. This is a very common structure too. Let's say we have a random variable representing the state of a system at time t, and let's say the state of the system predicts what the next state will be. Therefore, we can ask about the probability distribution of the current state of the system given the previous state $P(X_t \mid X_{t-1})$ where t and $t-1$ denote the time.

Next, let's say that, at every time step, our hypothetical system can generate a value, or in other words, we can make an indirect observation about the system. This observation is not the state of the system but something directly depending on it. So it is legitimate to ask for the probability $P(O_t \mid X_t)$, where O is the observation, depending on the state. Finally, putting things together in a bigger graph, we have the following:

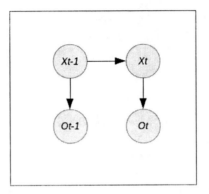

This graph has several names, depending on the types of the random variables X and O. When the variables are discrete, as we saw many times before, this model is also called a **Hidden Markov Model** — that is, a **Markov Model** in which the state is not directly observable (hidden). A Markov model is a model whose current states depend only on the previous state of the system. In this graph, it is clearly captured by the fact that X_t only depends on X_{t-1}. When all the variables follow a Gaussian distribution (and not a discrete one), this model is very famous: it is a Kalman filter!

So what's remarkable about probabilistic graphical models is that legacy models can also be represented by a graphical model.

You must remember that such a graph, when the edges are directed (arrows), cannot have a cycle. From a philosophical point of view, it means a consequence could be the cause of its cause, which is paradoxical. It means also that you would have an incomplete formula to represent the factorization of your probability distribution, and this is mathematically false in fact. For example, you cannot write $P(ABC) = P(A \mid B)P(B \mid C)P(C \mid A)$.

In the next section, we will see how we can compute any posterior distribution given any other variables in any type of graph. But before, let's have a look at a final graph, which is a combination of what we learned before:

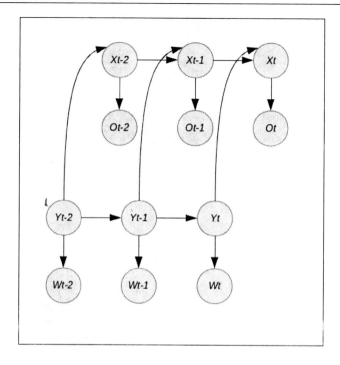

This graph is very interesting in the sense that it combines two Hidden Markov models together within the same model. But one of the models, Y, is also considered as a cause of the state of the other model, X. This is a very powerful combination. We can finally perform the reverse exercise and write the join probability distribution for this graph:

$$P(\chi) = P(Y_{t-2}).P(W_{t-2}|Y_{t-2})$$
$$P(Y_{t-1}|Y_{t-2}).P(W_{t-1}|Y_{t-1})$$
$$P(Y_t|Y_{t-1}).P(W_t|Y_t)$$
$$P(X_{t-2}|Y_{t-2}).P(O_{t-2}|X_{t-2})$$
$$P(X_{t-1}|Y_{t-1},X_{t-2}).P(O_{t-1}|X_{t-1})$$
$$P(X_t|Y_t,X_{t-1}).P(O_{t-1}|X_{t-1})$$

Variable elimination

The previous example is quite impressive and seems to be complex. In the following sections we are going to see how to deal with such complex problems and how to perform inference on them, whatever the model is. In practice, we will see that things are not as idyllic as they seem to be and there are a few restrictions. Moreover, as we saw in the first chapter, when one solves the problem of inference, one has to deal with the NP-hard problem, which leads to algorithms that have an exponential time complexity.

Nevertheless there are dynamic programming algorithms that can be used to achieve a high degree of efficiency in many problems of inference.

We recall that inference means the computing of a posterior distribution of a subset of variables, given observed values of another subset of the variables of the model. Solving this problem in general means we can choose any disjoint subsets.

Let χ be the set of all the variables in the graphical model and let Y and E be two disjoint subsets of variables $Y, E \subset \chi$. We will use Y as the query subset, that is, the variables we want to know the posterior distribution about, and E as the observation subset, that is, the variables for which we have an observation, also called an evidence (hence the E).

Therefore the general form of a query is $P(Y \mid E = e) = P\dfrac{(Y,e)}{p(e)}$ according to the Bayes theorem, as seen in *Chapter 1, Probabilistic Reasoning*. In fact, $P(Y,e)$ can be considered as a function on Y such that $P(Y, E = e) \rightarrow P(y, e) = P(Y = y, E = e)$ — that is, the probability of having $Y=y$ and $E=e$ at the same time.

Finally, we can define W by $W = \chi - Y - E$ — that is, the subset of variables in the graphical model that are neither considered for the query, nor observed. Then we can compute by $P(y, e) = \sum_{w \in W} p(y, e, w)$. Indeed if we marginalize over the variables in W, we are left with $P(Y,E)$.

If we apply the same reasoning, we can also compute the probability of the evidence $P(E=e)$, such as for example $P(e) = \sum_y P(Y, e)$.

Therefore the general mechanism for Bayesian inference is to marginalize over the unwanted and observed variables to be left with the query's variables.

Let's take a simple example with the following graph:

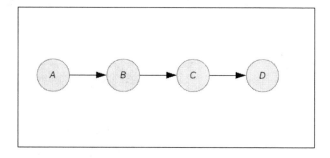

This graphical model encodes the probability distribution:

$$P(ABCD) = P(A).P(B\,|\,A).P(C\,|\,B).P(D\,|\,C)$$

It is a very simple chain that will serve the purpose of our presentation of the variable elimination algorithm. To each node of the graph, as we saw before, we associate a potential function, which in the case of a directed graphical model such as this one is simply the conditional probability of the variable given its parents: $P(A)$, $P(B\,|\,A)$, $P(C\,|\,B)$ and $P(D\,|\,C)$. If $P(A)$ can be directly read from the graph's associated functions, $P(B)$ has to be computed by marginalizing over A:

$$P(B) = \sum_a P(B\,|\,a)P(a).$$

It looks simple but it can become a very computing-intensive operation to run (OK, not that much but you get the point). If $A \in \mathbb{R}^k$ and $B \in \mathbb{R}^m$ (that is, A is a variable with k possible values and B with m values), doing the previous sum requires $2m.k - m$ operations. To understand this we can write the sum:

$$P(B = i) = \sum_a P(a)P(B = i\,|\,a)$$
$$= P(A = 1)P(B = 1\,|\,A = 1) +$$
$$P(A = 2)P(B = 1\,|\,A = 2) +$$
$$\cdots$$
$$P(A = k)P(B = 1\,|\,A = k)$$

And this has to be computed for each and every m value of B.

After doing this operation, we marginalized out A and we could say that we obtained an equivalent graphical model such as this one:

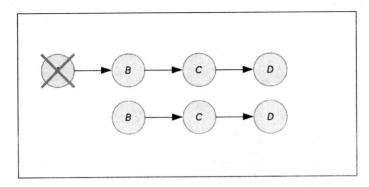

Here, the distribution of B has been updated with the information from A. If we want to find the marginal distribution of C, we can apply the same algorithm again and obtain $P(C)$. And again if we want to obtain $P(D)$. So in the end, what we've done, in order to obtain $P(D)$, is the following summations:

$$P(D) = \sum_c \sum_b \sum_a P(A).P(B \mid A).P(C \mid B).P(D \mid C)$$

However. because in each summation we only need to address the concerned variables in the sum. we can rewrite the sum as:

$$P(D) = \sum_c P(D \mid C) \sum_b P(C \mid B) \sum_a P(A).P(B \mid A)$$

This considerably simplifies the computations because they have to be done on local distributions only. As an exercise, I will let the reader show that for a graphical model representing a chain of n variables in $\mathbb{R}^k$ then the complexity of the computations goes from $O(k^n)$ to only. Remember that the big O notation means the upper bound of the computation time is proportional to the formula in the parentheses of the O function (also called the worst-case time complexity). Obviously, this scheme is efficient.

The main scheme that appears in this example is that we can sum variables out and then reuse the result for the next step. Ideally, we want to apply the same idea to any graph and eliminate variables step by step by caching intermediate results to use them again. This can be achieved because, thanks to the structure of the graphical model, each sub-expression in the summation only depends on a few variables and because we can cache the results along the path in the graph.

Sum-product and belief updates

When computing the distribution of one variable (or a subset of variables), the main operation is the marginalization, which consists of summing over a variable (or a subset of variables) to eliminate it from the main expression. If we call φ a factor in the factorization of the joint distribution, we can use the following properties to generalize and improve the variable elimination algorithm we saw in the previous section:

- **Commutativity:** $\varphi_1\varphi_2 = \varphi_2\varphi_1$

- **Associativity:** $(\varphi_1\varphi_2).\varphi_3 = \varphi_1.(\varphi_2.\varphi_3)$

- And if $X \notin \varphi_1 : \sum_X (\varphi_1.\varphi_2) = \varphi_1 \sum_x \varphi_2$

If again we apply it to the joint distribution $P(ABCD)$ from the previous section, we again obtain:

$$P(D) = \sum_C \sum_B \sum_A \varphi_A\varphi_B\varphi_C\varphi_D$$
$$\sum_C \sum_B \varphi_C\varphi_D \left(\sum_A \varphi_A\varphi_B \right)$$
$$\sum_C \varphi_D \left(\sum_B \varphi_C \left(\sum_A \varphi_A\varphi_B \right) \right)$$

In the end, the main expression that comes again and again is the sum-product over a factor, which can be written as $\sum_Z \prod_{\varphi \in \Phi} \varphi$.

So in general, if we can find a good ordering of the factors or the variables in the case of a directed graphical model as we saw until now, we can, by applying the previous sum-product formula, eliminate step by step each variable until we obtain the desired subset.

The ordering must marginalize out each factor containing the variable that has to be eliminated, leading to a new reduced factor that will be used again.

One possible way to perform that is with the following algorithm (in *Probabilistic Graphical Models*, D. Koller, and N. Friedman, 2009, MIT Press), called the **sum-product variable elimination algorithm**:

- Φ: the set of factors
- Z: the set of variables to be eliminated
- ≺: ordering on Z

1. Let $Z_1, \ldots, Z_k$ be an ordering on Z such that $Z_i \prec Z_j \text{ iff } i < j$:
2. for i=1,...,k
3. $\Phi = SumProductEliminateVar\left(\Phi, Z_i\right)$
4. $\varphi^* = \prod_{\varphi \in \Phi} \varphi$
5. return φ^*

This algorithm does the following: after receiving an order for eliminating variables or factors step after step, for each variable (or factor) it applies the algorithm to eliminate the variable and reduces the set of factors with the results from this function (defined next). Then it multiplies the remaining factors and returns the result.

The sub-procedure is as follows and aims at eliminating one variable at a time:

SumProductEliminateVar Algorithm(

Φ: set of factors,

Z: variable to be eliminated)

1. $\Phi' = \varphi \in \Phi : Z \in Scope\left(\varphi\right)$
2. $\Phi'' = \Phi - \Phi'$
3. $\Psi = \prod_{\varphi \in \Phi'} \varphi$
4. $\tau = \sum_Z \psi$
5. return $\Phi'' \cup \{\tau\}$

The second procedure does exactly what we have been doing step by step in the previous examples. The idea is to first multiply the potential in which the variable Z occurs and then marginalize out (line 4) to eliminate the variable Z. Finally, the algorithm returns the set of factors in which all the factors containing Z have been removed (line 2) and the new sum-product factor resulting from the marginalization of Z has been added (line 5). Also note that the first line selects all the factors that contain the variable Z to be eliminated.

So finally, when this procedure is applied sequentially to an ordering of the variables, one can eliminate them one after another until the desired subset is obtained.

Let's see how it works on an example where the graphical model is again as follows:

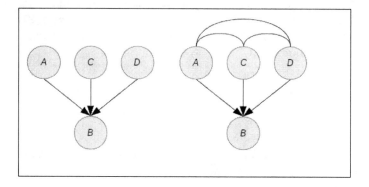

This is a factorization: $P(ABCD) = P(A).P(B|A).P(C|B).P(D|B)$ and the conditional distribution (factors) are defined by the following matrices:

```
A=matrix(c(.8,.2),2,1)
B=matrix(c(.6,.4,.3,.7),2,2)
C=matrix(c(.5,.5,.8,.8),2,2)
D=matrix(c(.3,.7,.4,.6),2,2)
```

The conditional distributions are represented as columns in the matrix. For example, B is:

```
      [,1]  [,2]
[1,]  0.6   0.3
[2,]  0.4   0.7
```

The set of variables to be eliminated is $\{A,B,C\}$ so that in the end we obtain the marginal probability distribution of D. So we are going to apply the algorithm step by step:

6. We begin by eliminating A in order to obtain $P(B,C,D)$ and so we need to marginalize A out:

$$A^T.B^T = \begin{pmatrix} 0.8 & 0.2 \end{pmatrix} \times \begin{pmatrix} 0.6 & 0.4 \\ 0.3 & 0.7 \end{pmatrix} = \begin{pmatrix} 0.48+0.06 \\ 0.32+0.14 \end{pmatrix} = \begin{pmatrix} 0.54 \\ 0.46 \end{pmatrix} = B^*$$

7. We continue by eliminating B to obtain $P(C,D)$ by performing the same procedure, this time reusing the previous result. Indeed in line 3 of the first algorithm, you can see that the result of calling SumProductEliminateVar with parameter Φ is assigned to Φ again. That's what we are doing here by using the previous result:

$$B^{*T}.C^T = \begin{pmatrix} 0.54 & 0.14 \end{pmatrix} \times \begin{pmatrix} 0.5 & 0.5 \\ 0.8 & 0.2 \end{pmatrix} = \begin{pmatrix} 0.638 \\ 0.362 \end{pmatrix} = C^*$$

8. At this point we are left with only two variables C and D, and we need to eliminate C using again the same procedure as described in the second algorithm:

$$C^{*T}.D^T = \begin{pmatrix} 0.638 & 0.362 \end{pmatrix} \times \begin{pmatrix} 0.3 & 0.7 \\ 0.4 & 0.6 \end{pmatrix} = \begin{pmatrix} 0.3362 \\ 0.6638 \end{pmatrix} = P(D)$$

In R you can quickly check the result by carrying out the following code:

```
Bs = t(A) %*% t(B)
Cs = Bs %*% t(C)
Ds = Cs %*% t(D)
Ds
          [,1]      [,2]
[1,] 0.3362 0.6638
```

In the end, we are left with three questions:

- If I observe a variable, how can I compute the posterior probability of another subset of variables?

- Is it possible to automatically find an optimal (or at least very efficient) ordering of the variables?

- If such an ordering exists, can we apply it to any type of graph, especially graphs with loops (loops but not cycles, as explained before)?

The answer to the first question is remarkably simple as the only operation to perform is to replace each factor φ by the instantiation of $\varphi[E = e]$. But if we only apply the previous algorithm such as this, we will obtain $P(Z, e)$ if Z is the query subset. So one needs to normalize again, according to the Bayes formula, to obtain the conditional posterior probability as desired.

The previous algorithm must be extended as follows:

- $\alpha = \sum_{z \in Val(Z)} \varphi^*(y)$ where $\varphi^* = P(Z, e)$ is the marginal distribution previously computed

- $P(Y \mid e) = \dfrac{P(Y, e)}{P(e)} = \dfrac{\varphi^*}{\alpha}$

We will answer to the second and third section of this chapter with a new algorithm called the junction tree algorithm, which is the most fundamental algorithm to date in the field of probabilistic graphical models. Its purpose is to transform any graph into a tree of clustered variables such that it is possible to apply the previous algorithm with an optimal ordering, minimizing the computational costs.

The junction tree algorithm

In this section we will have an overview of the main algorithm in probabilistic graphical models. It is called the junction tree algorithm. The name arises from the fact that, before performing numerical computations, we will transform the graph of the probabilistic graphical model into a tree with a set of properties that allow the efficient computation of posterior probabilities.

One of the main aspects is that this algorithm will not only compute the posterior distribution of the variables in the query, but also the posterior distribution of all other variables that are not observed. Therefore, for the same computational price, one can have any posterior distribution.

In order to achieve such a result, the junction tree algorithm will combine the efficiency of belief propagation and the sum-product as we saw before and the generality of the variable elimination procedure. Indeed, variable elimination works on any type of tree (but not on graphs with loops) and the sum-product caches intermediary results in order to make the computations more efficient. Because variable elimination only works on trees, we need to transform a graph with loops into a tree representing an equivalent factorization of the distribution.

The junction tree algorithm is based on the following consideration. Let's take our favorite example again $P(A, B, C, D) = P(A)P(B \mid A)P(C \mid B)P(D \mid C)$ and apply the Bayes rule to each factor:

$$P(A, B, C, D) = P(A) \cdot \frac{P(A, B)}{P(A)} \cdot \frac{P(B, C)}{P(B)} \cdot \frac{P(C, D)}{P(D)} = \frac{P(A, B) \cdot P(B, C) \cdot P(C, D)}{P(B)P(D)}$$

This formula is very interesting because we use as the denominator the variables in the intersection of the sets {A,B},{B,C} and {B,C},{C,D}. This reparameterization of the initial factorization is a prime indicator of how to transform a graph and how to perform inference on this transformed graph. Indeed, P(B) and P(D) are the probability distribution of the separator between the aforementioned sets — that is, the intersection of some clusters of the variable.

Of course, this is not the general principle but a useful observation for building a tree from a graph and performing inference.

The building of a junction tree will go through four phases in order to transform the graph into a tree:

1. Moralization of the graph, which consists in joining each pair of parents of each node with an undirected edge:

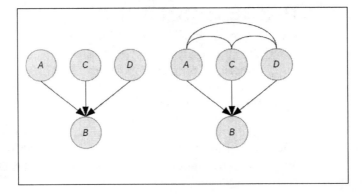

2. Then the graph is transformed into an undirected graph where each arrow is replaced by a simple edge. The effect of the first two operations is that each variable (a node in the graph) and its parent are now in the same clique — that is, a subgraph where the nodes are all connected.

3. Then the graph is triangulated: when a graph has loops, the results from variable elimination and re-representation in terms of the induced graph is equivalent to adding an edge between two variables belonging to the same undirected loop. We saw a simple example before: we eliminated variable A and obtained a new graph. When a graph has a loop this elimination step is equivalent to adding a cord between two nodes and we therefore need to perform it in the graph before the next step. In the next graph, the dashed lines are due to triangulation, while the plain lines are due to the two previous steps:

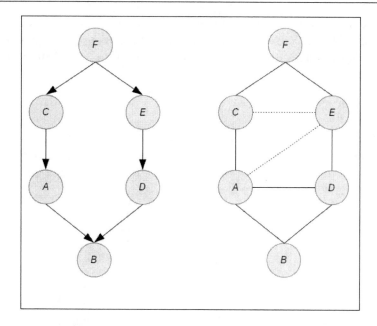

4. Finally, the last step will transform the triangulated graph into a cluster tree in which each node represents a factor on a subset of variables. The subset is determined by each clique of the graph. In between each cluster node, we will have another type of node called the separator. Recall the first simple example we saw at the beginning of this section, in which we reparameterized the model by putting a the denominator all the separators: this is exactly what we're performing here, but on any type of graph. The cluster tree is calculated by:

    ◦ Finding each clique of the triangulated graph and joining the nodes from those cliques into a single node.

    ◦ Computing a maximum spanning tree on the graph. The junction tree is this maximum spanning tree.

So from the cluster tree we obtain at the end, which is also called a junction tree, we have two types of nodes: cluster nodes and separator nodes. More generally, in the same spirit as our initial example, the probability distribution of a junction tree is equal to:

$$P(\chi) = \frac{\prod_{c \in C} \varphi(c)}{\prod_{s \in S} \varphi(s)}$$

where $\varphi(c)$ is a factor on each cluster of the junction tree and $\varphi(s)$ is a factor on each separator of the junction tree. Let's look at the full transformation from an example in *Bayesian Reasoning and Machine Learning*, D. Barber, Cambridge University Press, 2012.

The initial graph is as follows:

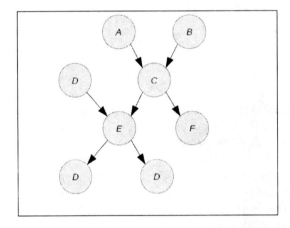

Now, the triangulated and undirected graph based on this initial graph is as follows:

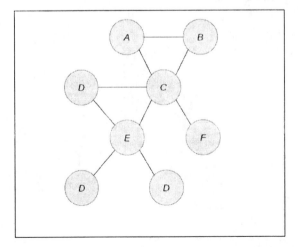

Finally, the junction tree is as follows:

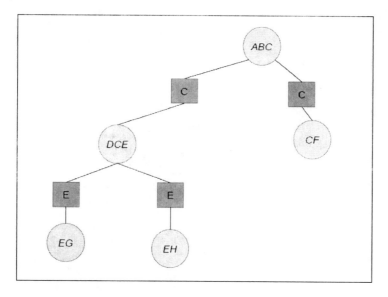

Inference on the junction is realized by passing messages from one cluster to the next one in two passes: from the root to the bottom and then the bottom to the root. After this full schedule of updates between clusters, each cluster will contain the posterior probability distribution of the variables it contains (such as for example *P(ABC)* in the top node in our example). Finally, finding the posterior distribution of any variables boils down to applying the Bayes rule on one of these clusters and marginalizing out the few variables we are not interested in.

Implementing a junction tree algorithm is a complex task, but fortunately several R packages contain a full implementation. And you already used them. Indeed, in the first chapter we saw small examples of Bayesian inference with the gRain package. The inference algorithm is the junction tree algorithm.

So as an exercise, we will build on and experiment with one of our previous examples in which we have variables *A*, *B*, *C*, *D*, *E*, and *F*. We will consider for the sake of simplicity that each variable is binary so that we won't have too many values to deal with. We will assume the following factorization:

$$P(ABCDEF) = P(F).P(C|F).P(E|F).P(A|C).P(D|E).P(B|A,D)$$

This is represented by the following graph:

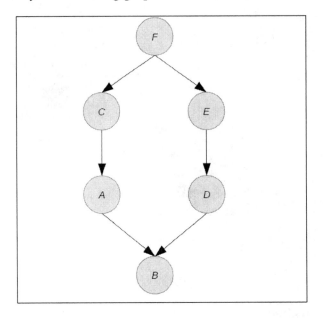

We first start by loading the gRain package into R:

```
library(gRain)
```

And then we create our set of random variables from *A* to *F*:

```
val=c("true","false")
F = cptable(~F, values=c(10,90),levels=val)
C = cptable(~C|F, values=c(10,90,20,80),levels=val)
E = cptable(~E|F, values=c(50,50,30,70),levels=val)
A = cptable(~A|C, values=c(50,50,70,30),levels=val)
D = cptable(~D|E, values=c(60,40,70,30),levels=val)
B = cptable(~B|A:D, values=c(60,40,70,30,20,80,10,90),levels=val)
```

As you may remember, the cptable function creates a conditional probability table, which is a factor for discrete variables. The probabilities associated to each variable are purely subjective and only serve the purpose of the example.

Because we have been giving the parents of each variable every time we created a conditional probability table, we also have defined our graph completely. Therefore, the next step is to compute the junction tree. In most packages, computing the junction tree is done by calling one function because the algorithm just does everything at once:

Here we will perform the following:

```
plist = compileCPT(list(F,E,C,A,D,B))
plist
```

We check the list of variables has been correctly compiled into a probabilistic graphical model and we obtain it from the previous code:

```
CPTspec with probabilities:
 P( F )
 P( E | F )
 P( C | F )
 P( A | C )
 P( D | E )
 P( B | A D )
```

This is indeed the factorization of our distribution as stated before. If we want to check further we can look at the conditional probability table of a few variables:

```
print(plist$F)
print(plist$B)
```

The result is, as expected, the conditional probability table:

```
F
 true false
0.1    0.9
, , D = true


       A
B        true false
  true    0.6   0.7
  false  0.4   0.3


, , D = false


       A
B        true false
  true    0.2   0.1
  false  0.8   0.9
```

The second output is a bit more complex but if you look carefully you will see that you have two distributions: *P(B|A,D=true)* and *P(B|A,D=false)*, which is a more readable presentation of *P(B|A,D)*.

We finally create the graph and run the junction tree algorithm by calling:

```
jtree = grain(plist)
```

Again, check the result we obtain:

```
jtree
Independence network: Compiled: FALSE Propagated: FALSE
  Nodes: chr [1:6] "F" "E" "C" "A" "D" "B"
```

At this point, you might think, "Is that all?" Well, yes it is. Now that you have the junction tree representation of the graph you can perform any possible inference. And moreover, you only need to compute the junction tree once. Then all queries can be computed with the same junction tree. Of course, if you change the graph, then you need to recompute the junction tree.

Let's perform a few queries:

```
querygrain(jtree, nodes=c("F"), type="marginal")
$F
F
  true false
  0.1   0.9
```

Of course, if you ask for the marginal distribution of *F*, you will obtain the initial conditional probability table, because *F* has no parents. At least we know it works!

```
querygrain(jtree, nodes=c("C"), type="marginal")
$C
C
  true false
  0.19  0.81
```

This is more interesting because it computes the marginal of *C* while we only stated the conditional distribution of *C* given *F*. We didn't need to have a complex algorithm such as the junction tree algorithm to compute such a small marginal. The variable elimination algorithm we saw earlier would be enough, too.

But if you ask for the marginal of *B* then variable elimination will not work because of the loop in the graph. However the junction tree will give the following:

```
querygrain(jtree, nodes=c("B"), type="marginal")
$B
B
    true     false
0.478564 0.521436
```

And we can ask for a more complex distribution, such as the joint distribution of *B* and *A*:

```
querygrain(jtree, nodes=c("A","B"), type="joint")
          B
A              true     false
   true   0.309272 0.352728
   false 0.169292 0.168708
```

In fact, any combination can be given such as A,B,C:

```
querygrain(jtree, nodes=c("A","B","C"), type="joint")
, , B = true


          A
C              true     false
   true   0.044420 0.047630
   false 0.264852 0.121662


, , B = false


          A
C              true     false
   true   0.050580 0.047370
   false 0.302148 0.121338
```

Now we want to observe a variable and compute the posterior distribution. Let's say F=true and we want to propagate down this information to the rest of the network:

```
jtree2 = setEvidence(jtree, evidence=list(F="true"))
```

And we query the network again:

```
querygrain(jtree, nodes=c("F"), type="marginal")
$F
F
 true false
 0.1   0.9
querygrain(jtree2, nodes=c("F"), type="marginal")
$F
F
 true false
     1     0
```

This query is most interesting: in the first query in `jtree` we have the marginal of *F* and in the second query in `jtree2` we have ... *P(F=true) = 1*!!! Indeed, we set an evidence in the network saying that *F=true*. So the probability is now 1 for this value.

More interestingly, we can ask for any joint or marginal now:

```
querygrain(jtree, nodes=c("A"), type="marginal")
$A
A
 true false
0.662 0.338
```

```
querygrain(jtree2, nodes=c("A"), type="marginal")
$A
A
 true false
 0.68  0.32
```

Here we see that knowing that *F=true* changed the marginal distribution on *A* from its previous marginal (the second query is again with `jtree2`, the tree with an evidence).

And we can query any other variable (and see that the results are different):

```
querygrain(jtree, nodes=c("B"), type="marginal")
$B
B
     true    false
```

```
0.478564 0.521436
```

```
querygrain(jtree2, nodes=c("B"), type="marginal")
$B
B
   true   false
0.4696 0.5304
```

Finally, we can set more evidences and propagate back and forth in the network to compute inverse probabilities as well:

```
jtree3 = setEvidence(jtree, evidence=list(F="true",A="false"))
```

Here we say that *F=true* and *A=false* and query the network again, looking at the difference between the before and after setting evidences:

```
querygrain(jtree, nodes=c("C"), type="marginal")
$C
C
 true false
 0.19  0.81
```

```
querygrain(jtree2, nodes=c("C"), type="marginal")
$C
C
      true      false
0.0989819 0.9010181
```

```
querygrain(jtree3, nodes=c("C"), type="marginal")
$C
C
    true    false
0.15625 0.84375
```

As expected, knowing a value for *A* and *F* drastically changes the probability distribution of *C*. As an exercise, I let the reader put an evidence of *F* (and then *F* and *B*) to see what happens to the posterior distribution of *A*.

Examples of probabilistic graphical models

In this last section we will show several examples of PGM that are good candidates for exact inference. The goal of this section is to show realistic yet simple examples of what can be done and to provide the reader with ideas for developing his or her own models.

The sprinkler example

This is an historical example which has been used in many textbooks. It is rather simple and shows a simple reasoning.

Let's say we look at our garden and see the grass is wet. We want to know why the grass is wet. There are two possibilities: either it was raining before or we forgot to turn off the sprinkler. Moreover, we can observe the sky. If it's cloudy, chances are it was raining before. However, if it was cloudy then presumably we didn't turn on the sprinkler, so it is more likely, in this case, we would have not forgotten to turn off the sprinkler.

This is a little example of causal reasoning that can be represented by a PGM. We identify four random variables: cloudy, sprinkler, rain, and wetgrass. Each of them is a binary variable.

We can give prior probabilities to each of them. For example, *P(cloudy=true) = P(cloudy=false)=0.5.*

For the other variables, we can set up conditional probability tables. For example, the *rain* variable could be defined as follows:

cloudy	P(rain=T | cloudy)	P(rain=F | cloudy)
True	0.8	0.2
False	0.2	0.8

We let the reader imagine what the other probability tables would be.

The PGM for this model is:

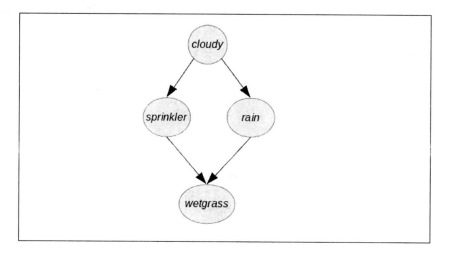

The medical expert system

One way to represent medical knowledge is to link symptoms to causes. The reasoning behind it is to say that causes will generate symptoms that can be observable. The problem is that there are many symptoms and many of them can have a common cause.

The idea of a PGM representing a medical knowledge base is to have two layers of nodes: one for the causes, and one for the symptoms.

The conditional probability tables associated with each node will strengthen or weaken the link between symptoms and causes so as to better represent the most likely cause of an observed symptom.

Depending on the degree of complexity of the associations, this kind of model can be a good candidate or not for exact inference.

Moreover, representing large probability tables can be a problem because there are too many parameters to determine. However, using a database of facts, it is possible to learn the parameters. In the next chapter we will see how to learn parameters.

The PGM is represented as follows:

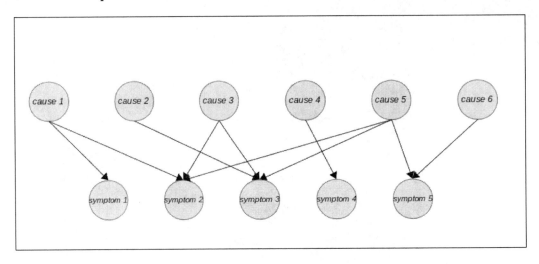

In this example, we see that **symptom 2** and **symptom 3** have three parents. In a more realistic medical model, it could be way more. For example, the headache symptom is caused by many different causes. In this case, it is not unusual to represent the conditional probability table associated with this node by an approximate version of it. One popular model is called the **Noisy-OR model**.

Models with more than two layers

Unlike the previous example, it makes sense in many applications to have a deeper causal reasoning and have causes and consequences layered on top of each other. It usually helps to understand the structure of the problem.

In these kinds of model, there is no theoretical limit to the complexity of the model, but we generally advise keeping the relationships simple between nodes. For example, it's a good practice for a node not to have more than three parents. If this is the case, then it is good to study the relationships in slightly more detail to see if, by any chance, the model could be decomposed a little further.

For example in J. Binder, D. Koller, S. Russell, and K. Kanazawa, *Adaptive Probabilistic Networks with Hidden Variables*. Machine Learning, 29(2-3):213-244, 1997, a model is developed for estimating the expected claim costs for a car insurance policyholder.

In this model a more layered approach is adopted to represent knowledge about car insurance. The following graph shows the model. Hidden nodes are shaded and output nodes are shown with heavy lines:

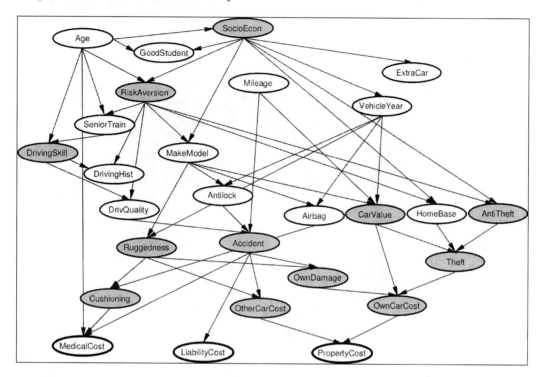

Sometimes, the model can become very complex, but is nevertheless still usable. For example in S. Andreassen, F. V. Jensen, S. K. Andersen, B. Falck, U. Kjærulff, M. Woldbye, A. R. Sørensen, A. Rosenfalck, and F. Jensen, *MUNIN - an Expert EMG Assistant. In Computer-Aided Electromyography and Expert Systems*, Chapter 21. Elsevier (Noth-Holland), 1989., a complex network has been designed.

We show here a representation taken from the bnlearn R package (http://www. bnlearn.com/) in which the PGM is particularly big.

The reader will note that the bnlearn R package is available on the CRAN repository and can be installed just like any other package.

The following figure shows the model developed in the aforementioned paper. The model has 1,041 nodes and 1,397 edges.

Obviously setting all the parameters by hand is impossible and this kind of PGM needs to be learned from data. But it is an interesting example of a complex model:

Tree structure

The tree-structured PGM is an interesting model because it usually leads to a very efficient inference. The idea is simply to model the relationship between variables such as a tree, where each node will have one parent but can have many children.

So for any variable in the model, we are always representing a simple relationship that can be encoded with $P(X \mid Y)$.

The following graph shows one example of such a model:

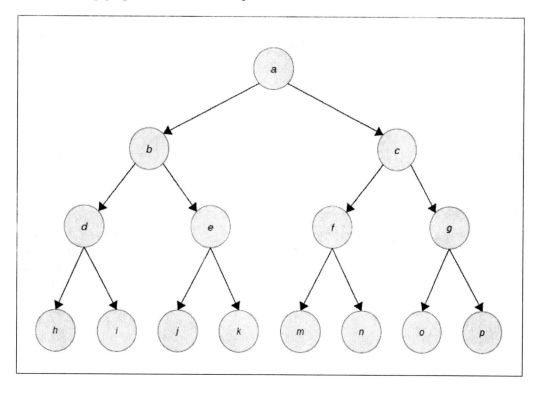

In this model, the clusters of nodes generated by the junction tree algorithm will always be made up of two nodes only: the child and its parent. So this model keeps the complexity of the junction tree algorithm low and allows for fast inference.

Of course, all these models can also be joined together to form more complex models if needed by the applications. These are just examples, and the reader is encouraged to develop his or her own models. One way to start is to understand what the causal relationships are between the variables of interest.

Also structural knowledge of the domain can be exploited to design new models. A step-by-step approach is always a good idea. One starts with a very simple model with just a few nodes and performs experiments with it to see if the model performs well. Then the model can be extended.

The problem of setting the parameters of such models is large and in the next chapter we will explore an algorithm to learn parameters from data, thus making it easier to develop an efficient PGM.

Summary

In the second chapter, we introduced the fundamentals of inference and we saw the most important algorithms for computing posterior distribution: variable elimination and the junction tree algorithm. We learned how to build a graphical model by considering causality, temporal relationships, and by identifying patterns between variables. We saw a fundamental feature of probabilistic graphical models, which is the combination of graphs to build more complex models. And we learned how to perform inference with a junction tree algorithm in R and saw that the same junction tree can be used for any type of query, on both marginal and joint distribution. In the last section we saw several real-life examples of PGM that can be used in many applications and are usually good candidates for exact inference.

In this chapter, we faced a problem when defining a new graphical model: the parameters are tedious to determine. In fact, even on small examples it's complicated. In the next chapter we will learn how to find parameters automatically from a dataset. We will introduce the **EM (Expectation Maximization)** algorithm and experiment with a complex problem: learning the structure of the graph itself. We will see that inference is the most important sub-routine of all learning algorithms, hence the necessity for having efficient algorithms such as the junction tree algorithm.

3

Learning Parameters

Building a probabilistic graphical model requires in general three steps: defining the random variables, which are the nodes of the graph as well; defining the structure of the graph; and finally defining the numerical parameters of each local distribution. So far, the last step has been done manually and we have given numerical values to each local probability distribution by hand. In many cases, we have access to a wealth of data and we can find the numerical values of those parameters with a method called **parameter learning**. In other fields, it is also called **parameter fitting** or **model calibration**.

Parameter learning is one important topic in machine learning. In this chapter we will see how we can use a dataset and learn the parameters for a given graphical model. We will go from the simple but common use case, in which the data is fully observable, to a more complex case, in which the data is partially observed, and therefore needs more advanced techniques.

Learning parameters can be done with several approaches and there is no ultimate solution to the problem, because it depends on the goal the model's user wants to reach. Nevertheless it is common to use the notion of maximum likelihood of a model and also maximum a posteriori. As you are now used to the notions of prior and posterior distribution, you can already guess what a maximum a posteriori could do.

In this chapter we will use datasets. When we have many variables in a model, at any time we can observe the value of those variables. Many observations of all the variables at the same time represent a dataset. For example, we have a model about a student's performance at University. In this model, we have several random variables such as the student's age, course, grade, gender, and year. A single observation could be *{21, Statistics, B+, female, 2nd year}*. And a dataset is a large collection of such observations.

Throughout this chapter, we will make the assumption that the dataset is *iid*, an acronym for **independently and identically distributed**. It means that each observation has been made using the same probability distribution and each observation is independent of all others in the dataset. As for the student's example it makes a lot of sense. But if we consider a time series dataset, such as the GDP of a country, then the dataset is not *i.i.d* anymore and different algorithms will be necessary to learn the parameters. As a matter of fact, *i.i.d* datasets cover a wide range of applications.

With all these notions in hand, we can now discuss the main topic in the chapter in a little more depth. Let's call D the dataset and θ the parameter of the graphical model. Then we call likelihood the function $P(D \mid \theta)$—in other words, the probability to observe (or generate) the dataset given the parameters. This is why probabilistic graphical models are sometimes called **generative models**.

A maximum likelihood estimation aims at finding the value of parameter θ, which maximizes the likelihood $P(D \mid \theta)$, and it is written as $\tilde{\theta} = argmax_\theta P(D \mid \theta)$. It is an optimization problem where one searches for the optimal value of θ, which maximizes $P(D \mid \theta)$.

If we want to be more precise about θ, we can adopt a Bayesian approach and also give a prior distribution over the parameters θ, $P(\theta)$. In this case, finding the parameter value boils down to finding the maximum value for $P(D \mid \theta).P(\theta)$. This is called a **maximum a posteriori**.

In this chapter, we will start by looking at simple examples of parameter estimation with a maximum likelihood and show how to implement them in R. Then we will look at the maximum likelihood estimation of a probabilistic graphical model. Finally, we will look at the harder estimation problem that occurs when data is missing, either randomly or when one has hidden variables. This will give us the opportunity to introduce one of the most important algorithms in machine learning: the E.M. algorithm. **E.M.** means **Expectation Maximization**.

The chapter will be structured as follow:

- An introduction with a simple example
- Learning as inference
- Maximum likelihood
- The EM algorithm

Introduction

In this chapter, we will learn how to make the computer learn about the parameters of a model. Our examples will use various datasets we will build ourselves or other datasets we will download from various websites. There are many datasets available online and we will use data from the UCI machine learning repository. These are made available by the Centre for Machine Learning and Intelligent Systems of the University of California, Irvine (UCI).

Iris photography from https://en.wikipedia.org/wiki/File:Iris_germanica_%28Purple_bearded_Iris%29,_Wakehurst_Place,_UK_-_Diliff.jpg

For example, one of the most famous datasets is the Iris dataset where each data point in the dataset represents the characteristics of an iris plant. Different attributes are used such as the sepal length/width and petal length/width.

It is possible to download this dataset and store it into a data.frame in R as we will do most of the time. Each variable is in a column and we will use *i.i.d* data (or assume they are in order) to simplify the calculus and computations.

Let's load the dataset first:

```
x=read.csv("http://archive.ics.uci.edu/ml/machine-learning-databases/
iris/iris.data",col.names=c("sepal_length","sepal_width","petal_
length","petal_width","class"))
head(x)
```

	sepal_length	sepal_width	petal_length	petal_width	class
1	4.9	3.0	1.4	0.2	Iris-setosa
2	4.7	3.2	1.3	0.2	Iris-setosa
3	4.6	3.1	1.5	0.2	Iris-setosa

4	5.0	3.6	1.4	0.2	Iris-setosa
5	5.4	3.9	1.7	0.4	Iris-setosa
6	4.6	3.4	1.4	0.3	Iris-setosa

As we see, each observation of the dataset is represented by one line in the dataset. It will be very useful later to use data.frame to simplify the computations of parameters.

We can do some simple estimation with this dataset. For example, if we consider only the first variable sepal_length and assume this variable follows a Gaussian distribution, then a maximum likelihood estimation of the two parameters of a Gaussian distribution (mean and variance) would simply be to compute the empirical mean and empirical variance. In R, it is as simple as that:

```
mean(x$sepal_length)
[1] 5.848322
```

```
var(x$sepal_length)
[1] 0.6865681
```

If we want to deal with discrete variables, as we will do in most of the chapter, we can use the well-known plyr package to simplify our computations:

```
library(plyr)
```

Now, we compute a distribution over the class variable in the data.frame by doing:

```
y = daply(x,.(class),nrow) / nrow(x)
y
       Iris-setosa    Iris-versicolor    Iris-virginica
        0.3288591         0.3355705         0.3355705
```

It is interesting to see the distribution of each class which is approximately 33% each. What we have done here is simply count the number of occurrences of each value in the column class of the data.frame and divide it by the total number of values. This gives a distribution and could also be used as prior probabilities on each class. In this case, our distribution would be roughly uniform.

If we go a bit further, we can also look at the distribution of another variable given a class. Let's assume that `sepal_length` is a Gaussian distribution with mean μ and variance σ². A simple joint distribution is given by the following factorization: $P(SepalLength, Class) = P(SepalLength | Class).P(Class)$.

Computing the conditional distribution *P(SepalLength | Class)* is the equivalent of computing all the mean and variance values for each value of the `class` variable. It is done by running:

```
daply(x,.(class), function(n) mean(n$sepal_length))
```

Iris-setosa	Iris-versicolor	Iris-virginica
5.004082	5.936000	6.588000

And similarly, the variances of each distribution conditioned on the `class` variable are given by:

```
daply(x,.(class), function(n) var(n$sepal_length))
```

Iris-setosa	Iris-versicolor	Iris-virginica
0.1266497	0.2664327	0.4043429

It is therefore very easy to compute conditional distributions using simple R functions. If we want to compute the same thing for discrete distributions, we could use the following code. First, let's transform the `sepal_width` variable into a discrete variable by discretizing it. It represents a width, so let's say we have three different values (for the sake of simplicity): {`small`, `medium`, `large`}. We can do that automatically with the following code:

```
q <- quantile(x$sepal_width,seq(0,1,.33))
```

We find the 33% and 66% quantiles of the variable `sepal_width`. Every value under 33% is `small`, every value between 33% and 66% is `medium`, and the rest over 66% are `large`.

```
q
   0%    33%    66%    99%
2.000 2.900 3.200 4.152
```

Then we create a new variable in the `data.frame`, the discretized version of `sepal_width`, by doing the following:

```
x$dsw[ x$sepal_ width < q['33%']] = "small"
x$dsw[ x$sepal_ width >= q['33%'] & x$sepal_width < q['66%'] ] = "medium"
x$dsw[ x$sepal_ width >= q['66%'] ] = "large"
```

For each interval as defined by the quantiles, we associate a value small, medium, or large to a new column in x called dsw (for **discrete sepal width**).

And finally, we can learn the conditional probability distribution *P(dsw | class)* by doing the following as before:

```
p1 <- daply(x,.(dsw,class), function(n) nrow(n))
```

```
p1
         class
dsw       Iris-setosa Iris-versicolor Iris-virginica
   large       36             5              13
   medium      12            18              18
   small        1            27              19
```

This gives us the count of each occurrence of each value of dsw when class has a specific value. If we want to transform it into probabilities, we need to divide each column by its sum. Indeed, each column represents a probability distribution by itself. This can be achieved by doing:

```
p1 <- p1 / colSums(p1)
```

And the result is finally:

```
         class
dsw           Iris-setosa       Iris-versicolor Iris-virginica
   large       0.7346939        0.1020408        0.2653061
   medium      0.2400000        0.3600000        0.3600000
   small       0.0200000        0.5400000        0.3800000
```

And by using the previous distribution over class we now have a fully parameterized model for the joint distribution: $P(SepalWidth, Class) = P(SepalWidth | Class).P(Class)$.

If we analyze what has been done and try to extract a rule of thumb, we can say that the parameters have been found by counting occurrences of values of sepal_width given each value of class. We can also say that we found the parameters of each factor of the distribution separately: once for *P(SepalWidth | class)* and once for P(class).

In the next sections, we will learn in a more formal way how we can generalize this notion to learn probabilistic graphical models with discrete variables and why, from a theoretical point of view, it works all the time.

Learning by inference

In the introduction to this chapter, we saw that learning can be done in a frequentist way by counting data. In most cases, it will be sufficient, but it is also a narrow view of the notion of learning. More generally speaking, learning is the problem of integrating data into the domain knowledge in order to create a new model or improve an existing model. Therefore, learning can be seen as an inference problem, where one updates an existing model toward a better model.

Let's consider a simple problem: modeling the results of tossing a coin. We want to test if the coin is fair or not. Let's call θ the probability that the coin lands on its head. A fair throw would have a probability of 0.5. By tossing the coin several times we want to estimate this probability. Let's say the ith toss outcome is $v_i = 1$ if the coin shows a head and 0 otherwise. We also assume there is no dependence between each toss, which means observations are *i.i.d.* And finally, we consider each toss as a random variable too. The joint distribution of a sequence is $P(v_1, v_2, ...v_n, \theta)$. Each toss is dependent on the probability θ, so the model is:

$$P(v_1,\ldots,v_n) = P(\theta)\prod_{i=1}^{N}P(v_i \mid \theta)$$

As a graphical model, this can be represented as shown in the following figures:

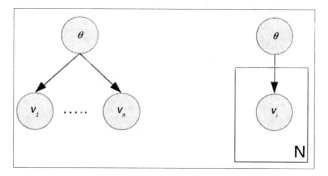

And it's about time we introduced a new notation term for graphical models: **the plate notation**. The left figure is our usual representation in which we only represent the first and the last of the v_i nodes, to make the figure simpler. This can sometimes be a bit confusing and in many cases ambiguous or cumbersome when one has too many nodes. The right side of the figure represents exactly the same graph where the box means that the node(s) inside are repeated N times.

In the previous section, we saw that learning integrates the data into the model and in the first chapter we saw that, using the Bayes formula, it was possible to update a probability distribution given new information. Applying the same principle, in our present problem we want to estimate the following probability:

$$P(\theta \mid v_1,\ldots,v_n) = \frac{P(v_1,\ldots,v_n,\theta)}{P(v_1,\ldots,v_n)} = \frac{P(v_1,\ldots,v_n \mid \theta)P(\theta)}{P(v_1,\ldots,v_n)}$$

This is a simple application, again, of the Bayes formula.

The next step is to specify the various factors of this formula, beginning with the prior $P(\theta)$. Intuitively, θ is a continuous variable because it should take any value between 0 and 1. However, we will simplify the problem and stay in the world of discrete variables only. Let's say θ can take three different values— unfair on both sides and fair; this is $\theta \in \{0.2, 0.5, 0.8\}$, and we give the prior probabilities:

$$P(\theta = 0.2) = 0.2 \quad P(\theta = 0.5) = 0.75 \quad P(\theta = 0.8) = 0.05$$

It means we believe that, with 75%, the coin is fair; with 20% it is biased toward the head; and with 5% it is biased towards the tail. The next step is to estimate the posterior distribution of θ as given earlier. Note that we will omit the denominator for the time being and use the symbol $\propto$, which means "is proportional to" with instead of a pure equality (=).

Therefore the posterior distribution can be estimated by:

$$P(\theta \mid v_1,\ldots,v_n) \propto P(\theta)\prod_{i=1}^{N} P(v_i \mid \theta) = P(\theta)\prod_{i=1}^{N} \theta^{I[v_i=1]}(1-\theta)^{I[v_i=0]}$$

This formula is not as complex as it seems. First we replace $P(v_1, \ldots ,v_n, \theta)$ by its decomposition as given with the graph. Then we replace $P(v_i \mid \theta)$ by its own expression, which is θ if $v_i = 1$ and $(1 - \theta)$ if $v_i = 0$. The function I [] is equal to 1 if the condition inside the brackets is true, and 0 otherwise; we use the fact that $x^0 = 1$.

I will let the reader finish the calculus and we finally obtain:

$$P(\theta \mid v_1,\ldots,v_n) \propto P(\theta)\theta^{\sum_{i=1}^{N} I[v_i=1]}(1-\theta)^{\sum_{i=1}^{N} I[v_i=0]}$$

The sums in this expression are simply the number of heads (resp. tails) in our experiment to see if the coin is fair. If we call these two sums N_{head} and N_{tail}, we can simplify our posterior on θ by doing:

$$P(\theta \mid v_1,\ldots,v_n) \propto P(\theta)\theta^{N_{head}}(1-\theta)^{N_{tail}}$$

So we can finally feed in this formula in R and look at the results of this Bayesian learning as an inference:

```
posterior <- function(prob,nh,nt, Theta=c(0.2,0.5,0.8))
{
        x=numeric(3)
        for(i in 1:3)
                x[i] = prob[i] * (Theta[i]^nh) * ((1-Theta[i])^nt)

        norm = sum(x)
        return(x/norm)
}
```

In this little function, `prob` is the vector of probability for each value of θ, `nh`, and `nt` are as defined just as before, and `Theta` is the vector of possible values for θ. We use the previously mentioned values by default. This code could be optimized but we preferred to keep it simple. The most important line is the one implementing our posterior formula. Then a normalization factor is the computer and the posterior probability distribution on θ is returned.

Let's play with this function to see what happens when different prior probabilities are given:

```
posterior(c(0.2,0.75,0.05),2,8)
[1] 6.469319e-01 3.530287e-01 3.948559e-05

posterior(c(0.2,0.75,0.05),8,2)
[1] 0.0003067321 0.6855996202 0.3140936477
posterior(c(0.2,0.75,0.05),5,5)
[1] 0.027643708 0.965445364 0.006910927

posterior(c(0.2,0.75,0.05),10,10)
[1] 0.0030626872 0.9961716410 0.0007656718

posterior(c(0.2,0.75,0.05),50,50)
[1] 5.432096e-11 1.000000e+00 1.358024e-11
```

We do the following experiments: 2 heads and 8 tails, 8 heads and 2 tails, 5 of each, 10 of each, and 50 of each. Note that the last experiment has a distribution summing to 1 due to errors in the exponentiation. This is something the reader should always test to debug his or her programs: a probability distribution, of course, always sums to 1. In this case, it means we reached the machine precision limit and errors occurred.

Let's analyze the results and see how we can solve this precision problem:

- **2 heads and 8 tails**: the coin is biased toward a small value for $\theta = 0.1$ with 65% of the chances. It means it's possible the coin is biased towards tails. But the fairness of the coin is still 35%, which is not small either.

- **8 heads and 2 tails**: we obtain the opposite results, but because our prior on the coin (being biased towards heads) was low $(P(\theta = 0.8) = 0.05)$, the result is still in favor of a fair coin with 68%.

- If we obtain an equal number of heads and tails, then the results are strongly in favor of a fair coin, increasing in probability when the number of experiments increases too.

Finally, here is a trick you must know when dealing with such probability computations. When you have to multiply a lot of small numbers like that, doing so uses logarithms and additions instead of regular values and multiplications. Therefore, the new algorithm will use the following equality: $log(ab) = log(a) + log(b)$. The new algorithm would therefore have the following change to compute $x[i]$:

```
x[i] = exp ( log(prob[i]) + nh*log(Theta[i]) + nt*log(1-Theta[i]) )
```

The last test we do is when the prior distribution is uniform — that is we give equal chances to each possible situation of the coin. Using our function we obtain:

```
posterior(c(1/3,1/3,1/3),2,8,c(0.2,0.5,0.8))
[1] 0.8727806225 0.1270062963 0.0002130812
posterior(c(1/3,1/3,1/3),8,2,c(0.2,0.5,0.8))
[1] 0.0002130812 0.1270062963 0.8727806225
posterior(c(1/3,1/3,1/3),5,5,c(0.2,0.5,0.8))
[1] 0.08839212 0.82321576 0.08839212
```

And we can see that the conclusion is moving to higher probabilities each time.

Maximum likelihood

This section introduces a simple algorithm to learn all the parameters of a graphical model as we saw until now. In the first section, we had our first experience of learning such a model and we concluded by saying that the parameters can be learned locally for each variable. It means that, for each variable x having parents $pa(x)$ in the graph, for each combination of the parents $pa(x)$ we compute frequencies for each value of x. If the dataset is complete enough, then this leads to the maximum likelihood estimation of the graphical models.

For each variable x in the graphical modeling, and for each combination c of the values of the parents of $pa(x)$ of x:

- Extract all the data points corresponding to the values in c
- Compute a histogram Hc on the value of x
- Assign $P(x \mid pa(x) = c) = H_c$

Is that it? Yes it is, it's all you have to do. The difficult part is the extraction of the data points, which is a problem you can solve in R using the `ddply` or `aggregate` functions.

But why is it so simple? Before looking at an algorithm in R, let's see why this algorithm works.

How are empirical and model distribution related?

A graphical model represents a joint probability distribution over a set of variables X. But not every joint distribution can be represented as a graphical model. Here we are interested in directed probabilistic graphical models as we defined them before. The definition can also be seen as a constraint on the type of probability distribution we want to represent and in this case the constraint is represented by:

$$P(X) = \prod_{i=1}^{K} P(x_i \vee pa(x_i)), X = x_1, \ldots x_N$$

So far, this is our well-known definition of a directed graphical model.

Definition: Empirical Distribution

Let $\chi = \{x_1, \ldots, x_N\}$ be a set of data points, which are states of a variable X, then the empirical distribution has its mass evenly distributed over the data points and zero elsewhere. Source: *Bayesian Reasoning and Machine Learning*, D. Barber 2012, Cambridge University Press.

From χ, assuming the data points are identically and independently distributed, the empirical cumulative distribution function is $\hat{F}(X) = \frac{1}{N}\Sigma_{i=1}^{N} I[X = x_i]$. In other words it is the distribution where, for each possible state of X, one associates the computed frequency from the dataset and as zero if no data is present in the dataset.

Let's consider the relationship between the empirical distribution $q(x)$ and the model distribution $p(x)$.

The Kullback-Leibler divergence (also called relative entropy) is a non-symmetric measure of the difference between two probability distributions, q and p, noted as $KL(q \mid p)$. It gives the expected number of bits required to transform a sample from q into a sample from p. Intuitively, if two distributions are equal then the Kullback-Leibler divergence is zero.

The KL divergence between the empirical distribution and a distribution $p(x)$ is:

$$KL(q \mid p) = \sum log\, q(x)q(x) - \sum log\, p(x)q(x)$$

The log-likelihood of the model $p(x)$ being $\sum_{i=1}^{N} log\, p(x_i)$, we can see in the previous formula that the right-most term is the expected log-likelihood of the model $p(x)$ under the empirical distribution $q(x)$. We can therefore write that:

$$KL(q \mid p) = \sum log\, q(x)q(x) - \frac{1}{N}\sum_{i=1}^{N} log\, p(x_i) + cst$$

And because the term $\sum log\, q(x)q(x)$ is not dependent on $p(x)$, the model distribution, we can consider it constant and write:

$$KL(q \mid p) = -\frac{1}{N}\sum_{i=1}^{N} log\, p(x_i) + cst$$

Therefore, as we know that maximizing the likelihood is equivalent to minimizing the log likelihood, from the previous formula, given that the second term is a constant, minimizing this log-likelihood will also minimize the KL divergence between the empirical distribution q and the model distribution p. It simply means that finding the maximum likelihood parameters for $p(x)$ is equivalent to minimizing the KL divergence between the empirical distribution and the model distribution.

If we have no constraint at all on $p(x)$, then the solution is to take $p(x)=q(x)$.

But recall that we have a few constraints: $p(x)$ has to be a graphical model. So now, let's put the real $p(x)$ from the graphical model into this formula to see what happens.

$$KL(q \mid p) = -\sum \left(\sum_{i=1}^{K} \log p\left(x_i \mid pa(x_i)\right) \right) q(x) + cst$$

Don't be scared by this double sum and just remember that $\log \prod_{i=1}^{K} p\left(x_i \mid pa(x_i)\right) = \sum_{i=1}^{K} \log p\left(x_i \mid pa(x_i)\right)$; that is, we only took the logarithm of the probability distribution of a graphical model. This huge term can be simplified by noting that the outer sum only depends for each term of the inner sum on the variable x_i, so we can now write:

$$KL(q \mid p) = -\sum_{i=1}^{K} \sum \log p\left(x_i \mid pa(x_i)\right) q\left(x_i, pa(x_i)\right) + cst$$

The inner sum now computes the expected log-likelihood under the distribution q restricted to the subset of variables x_i, $pa(x_i)$.

Now let's add back the constant to this formula:

$$KL(q \mid p) = \sum_{i=1}^{K} \left[\sum \log q\left(x_i \mid pa(x_i)\right) q\left(x_i, pa(x_i)\right) - \sum \log p\left(x_i \mid pa(x_i)\right) q\left(x_i, pa(x_i)\right) \right]$$

Again, this formula looks big, but inside the brackets, if you look carefully, you will recognize the formula of a KL divergence, this time between $q(x_i, pa(x_i))$ and $p(x_i, pa(x_i))$. This beautiful result means we can simplify this formula again with:

$$KL(q \mid p) = \sum_{i=1}^{K} \sum KL\left(q\left(x_i \mid pa(x_i)\right) \mid p\left(x_i \mid pa(x_i)\right)\right) q\left(pa(x_i)\right)$$

What we do in this final formula is a weighted sum of KL divergence. The probability distribution $q(pa(x_i))$ and the KL divergence both being positive, it happens that minimizing this sum corresponds with the minimization of each of its terms, because all of them are positive. And therefore, minimizing this sum also corresponds with the maximum likelihood estimation of $p(x)$ as we saw before. But if you look carefully at what is inside this sum, you will see more KL divergence, one for each little distribution associated with each node of the graph! And we have to minimize all of them. So it simply means that, if we want to minimize the whole KL divergence between q and p (and obtain the maximum likelihood estimation of p, our graphical model), we have to do the same thing on each node, independently of the other nodes, one by one. And minimizing all those KL divergences, as we saw before, is equivalent to counting and doing frequencies. Therefore, the maximum likelihood estimator for a directed graphical model is obtained by counting the data points (that is computing frequencies) on each node of the graph, by selecting only the data point associated with the parents of each node $pa(x_i)$.

The ML algorithm and its implementation in R

At this point, we are able to write a simple algorithm in R to learn the parameters of the graph. In this section we will use the `Nursery` dataset, again from UCI (https://archive.ics.uci.edu/ml/datasets/Nursery). The algorithm will not use any specific graphical model library but only the graph package and common R libraries.

The dataset has nine variables, related to nursery-school applications. The dataset was recorded in the 1980s in Ljubljana, Slovenia to rank applications to nurseries when the demand was too high, in order to build an expert system to objectively explain why an application was accepted or rejected. All the variables are categorical, which means we will only focus on discrete variables.

Our aim in this section is to illustrate what we have learnt so far in this chapter by application, so we will not try to make a perfect expert system. For this reason, we will use a simple graph to illustrate this example:

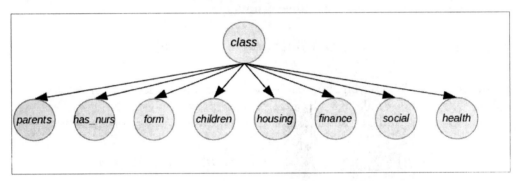

The R code is as follows, including the learning function where we use two new packages, `graph` and `Rgraphviz`. You will note that lines are numbered (but not part of the code), for ease of reading:

```
1 library(graph)

2 library(Rgraphviz)

3 library(plyr)

4

5 data0 <- data.frame(

6     x=c("a","a","a","a","b","b","b","b"),

7     y=c("t","t","u","u","t","t","u","u"),

8     z=c("c","d","c","d","c","d","c","d"))

9

10 edges0 <- list(x=list(edges=2),y=list(edges=3),z=list())
```

```
11 g0 <- graphNEL(nodes=names(data0),edgeL=edges0,edgemod="directed")
12 plot(g0)

13

14 data1 <- read.csv("http://archive.ics.uci.edu/ml/machine-learning-
databases/nursery/nursery.data", col.names=c("parents","has_nurs","form",
"children","housing","finance","so    cial","health","class"))
15 edges1 <- list( parents=list(), has_nurs=list(), form=list(),
children=list(),
16          housing=list(), finance=list(), social=list(),
health=list(),
17          class=list(edges=1:8) )
18 g1 <- graphNEL(nodes=names(data1), edgeL=edges1,edgemod="directed")
19 plot(g1)
```

From lines 1 to 3, we load the necessary packages. Then in line 5 we create a simple dataset to test the learning function. This dataset has three variables and will result in 50% probabilities for each combination.

In lines 10 and 11, we create the edges and the corresponding graph. In line 12, we plot the graph and obtain the following graphical model:

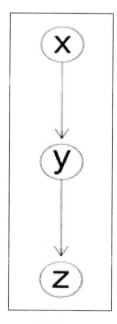

From lines 14 to 19, we instantiate a second graphical model, this time using the Nursery dataset. The output of the plot function is:

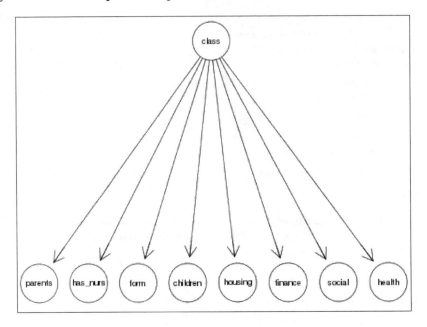

Next we have one simple function to compute the condition probability table for each variable with parents (or not):

```
1 make_cpt<-function(df,pa)
2 {
3       prob <- nrow(df)
4       parents <- data.frame(df[1,pa])
5       names(parents) <- pa
6
7       data.frame(parents,prob)
8 }
```

This function is in fact called later by the `ddply` function (the `plyr` package) and computes the frequency of one combination of the variable of interest and its parents. This is done is line 3 by a call to the `nrow` function.

The frequency here is only the number of times the same combination appears in the dataset. Because the combination is unique when this function is called (thanks to `ddply`), we extract the values of all the parents in line 4 from the first line only.

Finally, the main learning function is as follows. The code is not optimized but, on the contrary, is kept very explicit and simple so we can understand each piece:

```
1 learn <- function(g,data)
2 {
3       rg <- reverseEdgeDirections(g)
4       result <- list()
5
6       for(var in rg@nodes)
7       {
8           pa <- unlist(adj(rg,var))
9           if(length(pa)>0)
10          {
11              X <- ddply(data, c(var,pa), make_cpt, pa)
12              Y <- ddply(data, pa, make_cpt, pa)
13              for(i in 1:nrow(Y))
14              {
15                  c <- sapply(1:nrow(X), function(j) all(X[j,pa] ==
Y[i,pa]))
16                  c <- which(c)
17                  X$prob[c] <- X$prob[c]/Y$prob[i]
18              }
19          }
20          else
21          {
22              X <- ddply(data,var, function(df) c(prob=nrow(df)))
23              X$prob <- X$prob/sum(X$prob)
24          }
25
26          result[[length(result)+1]] <- X
27      }
28
29      return(result)
30 }
```

This function takes two parameters: the graph g and the dataset data. Then, in line 3, it reverses the direction of all edges, to be able to find the parents of each variable in line 8, using the function adj() from the graph package. There is nothing in the theory that says you have to reverse the graph; it's just a convenient way to find the parents.

In line 6, it will start to learn each variable independently, as we saw in the previous section. We deal with 2 problems, one when the variable has no parents (and therefore we compute the marginal distribution of the variable) and one when the variable has parents (and therefore we deal with conditional probability tables). See line 9.

In line 11, for each possible value of the variable and its parents, we compute *P(var,pa(var))* frequencies (counts is more accurate). In line 12, we do the same thing for *P(pa(var))*.

Finally, from lines 13 to 18, we apply the Bayes formula to obtain conditional probability tables and transform the counts into probabilities (or frequencies in this case, too). Lines 22 and 23 do the same thing for marginal probability tables.

The result for each variable is stored in a list called `result`!

So let's use this function with the two datasets to see the same results, and analyze them.

Application

First we load and run the previous code in R and then perform the following code:

```
learn(g0,data0)
```

The result will be:

```
[[1]]
  x prob
1 a  0.5
2 b  0.5


[[2]]
  y x prob
1 t a  0.5
2 t b  0.5
3 u a  0.5
4 u b  0.5


[[3]]
  z y prob
1 c t  0.5
```

```
2 c u  0.5
3 d t  0.5
4 d u  0.5
```

This tells us that $P(x = a) = 0.5$ and $P(x = b) = 0.5$. Looking at the dataset, we have an equivalent number of a and b for the variable x. This is good.

The other tables are for $P(y \mid x)$ and $P(z \mid y)$. Remember that conditional probabilities are not probabilities directly. These tables have to be read by values of the parents. For example $P(y = t \mid x = a) = 0.5$ and $P(y = u \mid x = a) = 0.5$. And the sum is obviously 1.

Now let's apply the `learn` function to the `Nursery` dataset and look at the results:

`learn(g1,data1)`

To simplify the output, we only show a few variables and start with `class`:

	class	prob
1	not_recom	3.333591e-01
2	priority	3.291921e-01
3	recommend	7.716645e-05
4	spec_prior	3.120611e-01
5	very_recom	2.531059e-02

This is a marginal probability table as expected from the graph we had before. The sum is 1 and we see that some values have higher probabilities than others. This one will be used in the expert system to make conclusions. Of course, our model is very simple and a more realistic model could have a different graph with different values. We encourage the reader to modify the graph `g1` to test different options.

If we look at the `finance` variable, we have the following table:

	finance	class	prob
1	convenient	not_recom	0.5000000
2	convenient	priority	0.5260197
3	convenient	recommend	1.0000000
4	convenient	spec_prior	0.4589515
5	convenient	very_recom	0.6646341
6	inconv	not_recom	0.5000000
7	inconv	priority	0.4739803
8	inconv	spec_prior	0.5410485
9	inconv	very_recom	0.3353659

This table is bigger than we saw before and behaves as expected. However, there is a small problem. This maximum likelihood procedure is by no means a Bayesian procedure but simply a frequentist. While it works in most cases, we can sometimes have problematic difficulties. Here, in line 3, we see that *P(finance = convenient | class =recommend) =1*.

While having a probability equal to one is not a problem, it is annoying. This is due to the fact that we only had one example of this specific combination in the dataset and this ended with this extreme result. This is not a desirable result as we want to be able to reach all possible scenarios and not fall into a unique scenario with probability 1.

We will see later in the book that it is interesting, in many cases, to add a prior distribution on all the parameters of the model, to prevent them from ever having a probability of 0 or 1 and to able to explore as many scenarios as possible.

Learning with hidden variables – the EM algorithm

The last part of this chapter is an important algorithm that we will use again in the course of this book. It is a very general algorithm used to learn probabilistic models in which variables are hidden; that is, some of the variables are not observed. Models with hidden variables are sometimes called latent variable models. The EM algorithm is a solution to this kind of problem and goes very well with probabilistic graphical models.

Most of the time, when we want to learn the parameters of a model, we write an objective function, such as the likelihood function, and we aim at finding the parameters that maximize this function. Generally speaking, one could simply use a black-box numerical optimizer and just compute the relevant parameters given this function. However, in many cases, this would be intractable and too prone to numerical errors (due to the inherent approximations done by CPUs). Therefore it is generally not a good solution.

We therefore aim at using the specificity of our optimization problem (alongside the assumptions made by a graphical model about the joint probability distribution) to improve our computations and make them fast and reliable.

The EM algorithm is a rather elegant solution to the problem of finding optimal parameters for a graphical model and it can be applied to many types of model.

Latent variables

Latent variables can be used in all models to, for example, introduce a level of simplification, to separate concepts, or to put some hierarchy into the models. For instance, we can observe a certain relationship between a set of variables, but instead of making all those variables dependent we would rather suppose that another hidden variable is simply the source of them and the dependency is done through this higher-level variable.

This top-down approach helps to make for simpler models, as in the following figure. This model is rather complex, isn't it ?

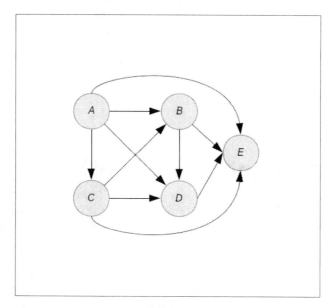

But if we add hidden variables (those with a Greek letter in the following figures), then the model becomes utterly simple and presumably tractable and easier to interpret. The problem is that we don't have data to estimate the probability distributions of the hidden variables and this is where we will need to use an EM algorithm.

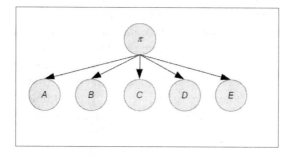

We can add more levels too to the model and group the variables with different parents, as illustrated in the following example:

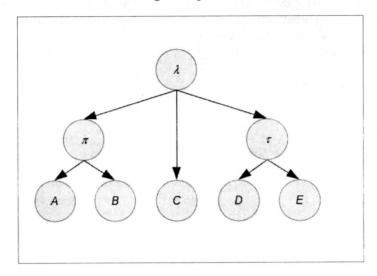

Principles of the EM algorithm

Because the latent variables are not observed, the likelihood function of such a model is a marginal distribution where we have to sum out (or integrate out) the hidden variables. Marginalization will create dependencies between the variables and make the problem complex to solve.

The EM algorithm deals with this problem essentially by filling-in missing data with their expected values, given a distribution. When we iterate this process over and over, it will converge to the maximum likelihood solution. This filling-in is achieved by computing the posterior probability distribution of the hidden variables given a current set of parameters and the observed variables. This is what is done in the E-step, (E for **Expectation**). In the M-step, **M** for **Maximization**, the parameters of the models are adjusted and we iterate again with a new E-step. We will go on until we see a convergence in the parameters, or a convergence in the growth of the likelihood. Moreover, the EM algorithm gives us the certainty that, after each EM step, the likelihood of the model cannot go down. It means that, when the likelihood only increases by a tiny amount, we can conclude that the algorithm converged to a (local) maximum and we can stop the algorithm. The tiny amount depends on the application but it's not unusual to stop when the likelihood hasn't moved by more than 10-2 to 10-4. It's just a rule of thumb and the reader is encouraged to plot the likelihood curve to better understand the EM algorithm's behavior for his or her special case.

Derivation of the EM algorithm

Let's assume we have a dataset D of N *iid* points and the parameters of the graphical models are called θ. At this point, if you're wondering what this θ is, it is a big variable containing all the parameters for every variable of the graphical model. As it would be tedious to write a long collection, we simply resume them in a single high-dimensional variable.

Let $D = \{x_1, ..., x_N\}$ and $\theta\ \varepsilon\ R$. The likelihood of the graphical model is defined by:

$$p(D|\theta) = \prod_{i=1}^{N} p(x_i | D)$$

In the complete case where all the variables are observed, the likelihood function can be decomposed as follow:

$$L(\theta) = \log p(D|\theta)$$
$$= \sum_{i=1}^{N} \log p(x_i | \theta)$$
$$= \sum_{i=1}^{N} \sum_{j=1}^{K} \log p\left(x_i^{(j)} | pa\left(x_i^{(j)}\right), \theta_i\right)$$
$$= \sum_{j=1}^{K} L_i(\theta_i)$$

We find again the result we saw before where the log-likelihood, in the case of a graphical model, can be rewritten as the sum of the local log-likelihood for each variable — that is, each node in the graph.

However, when we have hidden variables, we can't have this nice result. Let's call the observed variables x and the hidden variables y. The log-likelihood of the model can be written as:

$$L(\theta) = \log p(X|\theta) = \log \sum_{y} p(x, y|\theta)$$

Here, $X = \{x,y\}$ is the set of all the variables. And here is our main problem: the sum inside the *log* function is not nice to compute. In fact, in order to obtain the likelihood function we have to marginalize out the y hidden variable. And having this sum in the *log* function can potentially make all the variables inside it dependent on each other. Therefore, we would lose all the benefit of having a nice factorization thanks to using a graphical model. In the end, computing would become intractable.

But if we take any distribution $q(y)$ over the hidden variables, it can define a lower bound on the log-likelihood function. Let's see why:

$$L(\theta) = \log \sum_y p(x, y \mid \theta)$$

$$= \log \sum_y q(y) \frac{p(x, y \mid \theta)}{q(y)}$$

$$\geq \sum_y q(y) \log \frac{p(x, y \mid \theta)}{q(y)}$$

$$= \sum_y q(y) \log p(x, y \mid \theta) - \sum_y q(y) \log q(y)$$

$$= F(q, \theta)$$

This reasoning needs a bit of explanation now, line by line:

1. This is the standard definition of the log-likelihood over x where we marginalized out the hidden variables y.

2. Here we introduce $q(y)$ at the numerator and denominator so that they cancel out each other.

3. Thanks to this, we can apply the Jensen inequality to obtain a lower bound. The right-hand side formula is the lower bound on $L(\theta)$.

4. The lower bound is simplified again and we have two terms where the right-most term is independent of θ and x.

So in the end, this new function $F(q, \theta) \leq L(\theta)$ is the lower bound on the log-likelihood.

The way the EM algorithm works is by alternating optimizations in two steps:

*   **E-step:** $q_k \leftarrow argmax_q F(q, \theta_{k-1})$
*   **M-step:** $\theta_k \leftarrow argmax_\theta F(q_k, \theta_{k-1})$

The algorithm is usually initialized with a random set of parameters: θ_0.

What this algorithm does is first find a new marginal distribution over the hidden variable $q(y)$ given the current set of parameters θ_{k-1} and then it finds the maximum likelihood estimation of the parameters θ_k using the previous distribution q. So in fact, in step 1, the E-step, the maximum of q is obtained by setting $q_k(y) = p(y \mid x, \theta_{k-1})$. And, at this point, the lower bound becomes an equality:

$$F(q_k, \theta_{k-1}) = L(\theta_{k-1})$$

This result is very important because it guarantee that the likelihood can only go up or stay the same, step after step. So this result means that, using the current parameters θ_{k-1}, we infer the distribution $p(y \mid x, \theta_{k-1})$ given the other observed variables. Any inference algorithm can be used at this stage, like those we saw in the previous chapter. Moreover, this creates an expected complete set of observations given the current parameters.

The maximum in the M-step is obtained by maximizing the first term in line 4 of the previous derivation; that is, the expected log-likelihood under the distribution q, the one we just computed.

So, at the beginning of teach loop of the EM algorithm, we have $F=L$ and the E-step does not change θ. And so we know that the E-step will never decrease the likelihood. The log-likelihood will therefore only increase or stay the same. In practice, we will usually see a convergence of the log-likelihood. When the difference is very small, we can stop the algorithm and consider that the current solution is the good one.

Applying EM to graphical models

Practically we will consider a graphical model with discrete variables as we have been using so far. For example, let's say that somewhere in the graph we have two variables A and B, such that B is the parent of A. So locally we have the distribution $P(A \mid B)$ associated to node A.

We recall that the maximum likelihood estimate $\theta_{A|B}$ is computed by:

$$\theta_{A/B} = \frac{count\ of\ each\ combination\ of\ A, B}{count\ of\ each\ combination\ of\ B}$$

This is what we saw and implemented before in R. So far, nothing new. Remember, we used the `ddply` function to efficiently compute this in R in one call. You could also use the `aggregate` function to obtain the same result.

But this formula is only valid when A and B are fully observed! And here they are not. Therefore, using the EM algorithm to overcome this problem is very simple.

The M-step is in this case:

$$\hat{\theta}_{A=a|B=b} = \frac{\sum_{i=1}^{N} p\left(A = a, B = b \mid X = x_i\right)}{\sum_{i=1}^{N} p\left(A = b \mid X = x_i\right)}$$

But how do we obtain these two probability distributions? We obtain them in the E-step, using the observed X variables and our preferred inference algorithm. As for the parameters used in A and B, they are the parameters from the previous step of the EM algorithm.

In conclusion, in plain English, we recall the steps of the EM algorithm:

1. Initialize the graphical model with random parameters. Just be sure that the distribution sums to 1, of course. Random parameters seem to give better results than a uniform distribution, but I'm just giving you a practical tip here.

2. Until convergence of the log-likelihood, do the following:

    ○ **E-step**: Compute the posterior distribution, using your preferred inference algorithm, of all the hidden variables. This is the q distribution.

    ○ **M-step**: Compute the new set of parameters of the graphical model using the inferred distribution we saw before.

    ○ Update the log-likelihood and check whether it converged, usually by checking whether the difference between the current likelihood and the previous one is smaller than a predefined threshold.

And so the M-step acts as if the hidden variables were observed by using the expected distribution on it.

Summary

In this chapter we saw how to compute the parameters of a graphical model by using the maximum likelihood estimation.

The reader should note however that this approach is not Bayesian and could be improved by setting prior distributions over the parameters of the graphical models. This could be used to include more domain knowledge and help in obtaining better estimations.

When the data is not fully observed and variables are hidden, we learned how to use the very powerful EM algorithm. We also saw a full implementation of a learning algorithm in R for a fully observed graph.

We would like, at this point, to encourage the reader to use the ideas presented in this chapter to extend and improve his or her own learning algorithms. The most important requirement when doing machine learning is to focus on what is not working. From a dataset, any algorithm will, at some point, extract some information. However, when one focuses on the errors in an algorithm and where it does not work, one will really find value in the data.

In the next chapter, we will look at several simple, yet powerful Bayesian models that can be represented as graphical models. We will see that some of them can be highly optimized for inference and learning. We will also explore an application of the EM algorithm to find clusters in data, using Gaussian mixture models.

Bayesian Modeling – Basic Models

After learning how to represent graphical models, how to compute posterior distributions, how to use parameters with maximum likelihood estimation, and even how to learn the same models when data is missing and variables are hidden, we are going to delve into the problem of modeling using the Bayesian paradigm. In this chapter, we will see that some simple problems are not easy to model and compute and will necessitate specific solutions. First of all, inference is a difficult problem and the junction tree algorithm only solves specific problems. Second, the representation of the models has so far been based on discrete variables.

In this chapter we will introduce simple, yet powerful, Bayesian models, and show how to represent them as probabilistic graphical models. We will see how their parameters can be learned efficiently, by using different techniques, and also how to perform inference on those models in the most efficient way. The algorithms we will see are adapted to these models and take into account the specificity of each.

And, for the first time, we will start to use variables with continuous support—that is, random variables that can take any value as a number—and not just a finite number of discrete values.

We will look at simple models that can be used as a basic component for more advanced solutions. These models are fundamental and we will go from very simple things to more advanced problems, such as Gaussian mixture models. All these models are heavily used and have a nice Bayesian representation that we will present throughout this chapter.

More specifically, we will be interested in the following models:

- The Naive Bayes model and its extension, used mainly for classification
- The Beta-Binomial model, which is one of the most fundamental modelings
- Gaussian Mixture models, one of the most used clustering models

The Naive Bayes model

The Naive Bayes model is one of the most well-known classification models used in machine learning. Despite its simple appearance, this model is very powerful and gives good results with little effort. Of course, when considering the problem of classification, one should not always stay with one model, such as Naive Bayes, but should try out many examples to see which one is the best with a particular dataset.

Classification is an important problem in machine learning and it could be defined as the task of associating observations to a particular class. Let's say we have a dataset with *n* variables and we assign a class to each data point. The class could be *{0,1}* or *{a,b,c,d}*, *{red, blue, green, yellow}*, or *{warm, cold}*, and so on. We will see that it is sometimes easier to consider binary classification problems where one has only two classes. But most classification models can be extended to more than two classes.

For example, given physiological characteristics, we can classify animals into mammals or reptiles. Given the words used in an email, we can classify it as a junk email or a legitimate email. Given a credit record and other financial data, we can classify a client as trusted for a loan or not.

Just try the next little example to see a (not-so) obvious problem of classification.

```
Sigma <- matrix(c(10,3,3,2),2,2)
x1 <- mvrnorm(100,c(1,2),Sigma)
x2 <- mvrnorm(100,c(-1,-2),Sigma)
plot(x1,col=2,xlim=c(-5,5),ylim=c(-5,5))
points(x2,col=3)
```

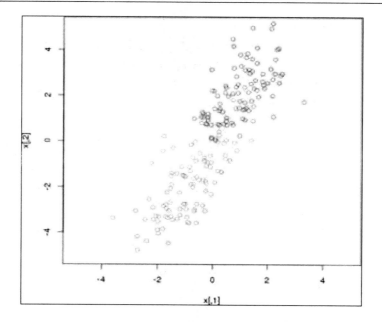

This example shows a two-variate classification problem with two classes, the red and the green. The two variables are represented as the x axis and the y axis. The problem seems obvious but it is not, because the interface between the red class and the green class is not clearly defined. This is typical of real-world problems.

In this case, we can still draw a clear line in the middle to separate the two classes. But sometimes it is not obvious and a line won't work. When a line can separate the two classes we call it **linear classification**. When we need a curvier separation, we call it **non-linear separation**.

The way we estimate the quality of a classifier is by looking at the error rate. We want the lowest error rate; that is, every time the classifier predicts a class for a data point, it has to be right. However, depending on the classification problem, the error can have a different consequence. For example, in a medical classification problem, classifying a patient as ill when he or she is not is presumably less dangerous than classifying the patient as healthy and letting him or her go with an undetected illness.

Obviously we want the classifier to be as accurate as possible and the general rule when building classifiers is to concentrate entirely on difficult cases.

Representation

The Naive Bayes model is a probabilistic classification model with N random variables X as features and one random variable C as the class variable. The main (and very strong) assumption made in this model is that, **given the class, the features are independent**. This seems to be very strong and surprisingly it gives good results in this situation.

The join probability distribution in the Naive Bayes model is:

$$p(X,C) = p(C)\prod_{i=1}^{N} p(X_i \mid C)$$

It is represented by the following graphical model:

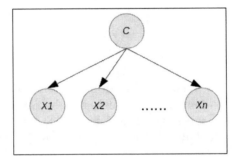

This is a very simple graphical model in fact and you can see from the graph why knowing the class will make all feature variables independent of each other.

Therefore, by using the Bayes rule, given a new data point X' we can compute the most probable class by doing:

$$p(c \mid X') = \frac{p(X' \mid C)p(C)}{p(X')} = \frac{p(X' \mid C)p(C)}{\sum_c p(X' \mid C)p(C)}$$

To make the problem simpler, we will interpret all the X_i variables, as well as the class variable C, as binary variables. However the theory stays the same if the variables have more than two possible values. In fact, the theory of this model is similar even if you consider continuous features too. For example, for real-value features, we can consider Gaussian distributions and have:

$$p(x \mid C = c) = \prod_{i=1}^{N} N\left(X_i \mid \mu_{ic}, \sigma_{ic}^2\right)$$

Here, N represents a Gaussian distribution.

When the features are binary the result is the same except that one uses the Bernoulli distribution for the X features:

$$p(x \mid C = c) = \prod_{i=1}^{N} N\left(X_i \mid \mu_{ic}, \sigma_{ic}^2\right) = \prod_{i=1}^{N} \theta_{ic}^x \left(1 - \theta_{ic}^{1-x}\right)$$

Here, x can take values in {0,1} and θ_{ic} is the probability for X_i to be one given class c.

Learning the Naive Bayes model

Learning a Naive Bayes model is extremely simple. Recalling what we saw in *Chapter 3, Learning Parameters*, it's very easy to infer that, for each θ_{ic}, in the case of binary features with a binary class variable, $\theta_{ic} = \dfrac{N_{ic}}{N_c}$ where N_{ic} is the count of 1 variable X_i when the class is $C = c$ and N_c is the count of class 1.

As for the class variable, it's even simpler: $\pi_c = N_c$ over N where N is the total number of data points.

The reason for that is the same as in the previous chapter. In order to understand why, we need to write the maximum likelihood of this model. For one data point, the probability is:

$$p(x_i c_i \mid \theta) = p(c_i \mid \pi) \prod_{j=1} N \, p(x_{ij} \mid \theta_j)$$

Knowing a class can take values in {0,1} only in the case of a binary classifier, we have therefore:

$$p(x_i c_i \mid \theta) = \prod_c \pi_c^c \prod_j \prod_c p\left(x_{ij} \mid \theta_{jc}\right)^c$$

And therefore the log-likelihood is

$$\log p(D \mid \theta) = \sum_{c=1}^{C} N_c \log \pi_c + \sum_{j=1} N \sum_{c=1}^{C} \sum_{i/c_i=c} \log p\left(x_{ij} \mid \theta_{jc}\right)$$

In order to maximize this function, we see that we can optimize each term individually, leading to the simple form we obtained for each parameter. So, naturally, it gives exactly the same results as general graphical models.

Instead of implementing the model manually, we will use an R package named `e1071`. If you don't have it yet, you can install and load it by doing:

```
install.packages("e1071")
library(e1071)
```

This provides a full implementation of the Naive Bayes model. We can now load data and look at some results:

```
data(iris)
model <- naiveBayes(Species~.,data=iris)


Naive Bayes Classifier for Discrete Predictors


Call:
naiveBayes.default(x = X, y = Y, laplace = laplace)


A-priori probabilities:
Y
    setosa versicolor  virginica
 0.3333333  0.3333333  0.3333333


Conditional probabilities:
          Sepal.Length
Y                [,1]       [,2]
  setosa        5.006 0.3524897
  versicolor    5.936 0.5161711
  virginica     6.588 0.6358796


          Sepal.Width
Y                [,1]       [,2]
  setosa        3.428 0.3790644
  versicolor    2.770 0.3137983
```

```
virginica   2.974 0.3224966
```

```
            Petal.Length
Y                 [,1]        [,2]
  setosa         1.462 0.1736640
  versicolor     4.260 0.4699110
  virginica      5.552 0.5518947
```

```
            Petal.Width
Y                 [,1]        [,2]
  setosa         0.246 0.1053856
  versicolor     1.326 0.1977527
  virginica      2.026 0.2746501
```

This example needs a bit of explanation. The `laplace` parameter controls the Laplace smoothing of the data, in order to help the model when data is not perfectly balanced or the dataset exhibits problematic situations. We will come back to this problem later, but it's one of the main problems one has to deal with in most classification problems.

By using this model and trying to predict (or infer) the class, we obtain the following:

```
p <- predict(model,iris)
```

```
hitrate <- sum(p == iris$Species) / nrow(iris)
```

And we obtain a hit rate of 0.96, as 96% of the data points were correctly classified. It's great but bear in mind that we use the training dataset to compute this percentage. You can't estimate the real power of a classification model using only data points you used to train the model. Ideally, we should split the dataset in two; let's say we will use 1/3 to test it and 2/3 to train the model. Ideally, the split has to be done randomly:

```
ni <- sample(1:nrow(iris),2*nrow(iris)/3)
no <- setdiff(1:nrow(iris),ni)
model <- naiveBayes(Species~.,data=iris[ni,])
p <- predict(model,iris[no,])
```

Here, `ni` and `no` are a list of data point indices taken at random from the initial dataset.

Bayesian Naive Bayes

This model, despite its name, is not a Bayesian model. To be fully Bayesian we should express prior on the parameters. In the Naive Bayes model, the parameters are those of the class variable π_c and those of the feature variables θ_i. These parameters have been estimated using a maximum likelihood method but what happens if the dataset is unbalanced? What will happen to the parameters if the dataset lacks enough points for a certain number of cases? We will end up with very bad estimators and in the worst case we will have zeros for the ill-represented parameters. This is obviously something we don't want because the results will be completely false, giving too much importance to the features' values or classes and none to the rest.

This problem is called **over-fitting**. And one simple solution to over-fitting is to use a Bayesian approach and include extra information in the model to say, "If the data is not represented, then let's assume it has a very small probability but not a zero probability."

One elegant and simple solution to this problem is to use prior distributions on the parameters of the model and develop the model in a Bayesian way. Let's make a few assumptions in order to simplify the calculus. First of all, we will assume that all the feature variables have the same finite number values. We will call this number S. You can easily generalize this to any number of values for each feature, but in our presentation it makes things simpler. Then we will assume we can use a factored prior on the θ feature parameters, as follows:

$$p(\theta) = p(\pi) \prod_{i=1}^{N} \prod_{c=1}^{C} p(\theta_{ic})$$

Here, θ represents all the parameters. In order to make it clear, we use the following notation:

- θ represents all the feature parameters and π the class parameters
- θ_i represents all the parameters of the variable i — that is, the parameters of the conditional distribution $p(X_i \mid C)$
- θ_{ic} represents all the parameters of the variable i — that is, the parameter distribution $p(X_i \mid C = c)$
- $\theta_{ic}^{(s)}$ represents the parameter of the probability $p(X_i = s \mid C = c)$ — that is, because X_i is a discrete multinomial variable (in fact it's more accurate to say categorical than multinomial here), $p(X_i = s \mid C = c) = \theta_{ic}^{(s)}$

And because we just mentioned multinomial distribution, it's important to note that the Dirichlet distribution is also the conjugate distribution for the multinomial (and the categorical) distribution. If we consider all the $\theta_{ic}^{(s)}$ to be random variables and no longer just simple parameters, we need to give them a probability distribution a priori. We will assume they are Dirichlet distributed for two reasons:

- The Dirichlet distribution is a distribution over a vector of values such that their sum is 1, which corresponds to the well-known constraint that $\sum_{s=1}^{S} \theta_{ic}^{(s)} = 1$. So far, nothing new.
- The Dirichlet distribution being the conjugate prior for the multinomial distribution, this means that, if a data point has a categorical or multinomial distribution and the prior distribution on the parameters is a Dirichlet (as in our case), then the posterior distribution on the parameters is also a Dirichlet. And this will simplify all of our computations.

In fact, contumacy is a very powerful tool in Bayesian data analysis.

In practice it works as follows:

- Let's say that α is the concentration parameter — that is, the parameter of the Dirichlet distribution $Dir(\alpha)$.
- So we assume that the θ's are distributed Dirichlet — that is $p(\theta_{ic} \mid \alpha) = Dir(\alpha)$.
- And, of course, we know that our feature variables have a categorical or multinomial distribution.
- Therefore the posterior probability of the parameters of the distribution of X_i after counting data (as we did before), will be a Dirichlet $Dir(N_i + \alpha)$, where N_i is the counts we did before! It's as simple as that, thanks to the conjugacy.

So finally, if we want to incorporate the Dirichlet prior into our computations, the posteriors of the parameters for the class variable are:

$$\pi_c = \frac{N_c + \alpha_c}{N + \alpha_0} \text{ where } \alpha_0 = \sum_c \alpha_c.$$

And the prior distribution of π is a $Dir(\alpha)$ where $\alpha = (\alpha_1, ..., \alpha_c)$.

For the parameters of the feature variables, the solution is exactly the same:

$$\theta_{ic}^{(s)} = \frac{N_{ic} + \beta_s}{N_c + \beta_0} \text{ where } \beta_0 = \sum_s \beta_s$$

And the prior distribution of θ_{ic} is a $Dir(\beta)$, where $\beta = (\beta 1, ..., \beta s)$.

Wait! Is it really as simple as this? Well, yes it is, thanks to the conjugacy in this Bayesian model. If you look carefully at the formulas, you will see that none of the π_c and $\theta_{ic}^{(s)}$ can be equal to zero now because of the values of α and β. Indeed, in the definition of the Dirichlet distribution, it is required that the parameters of the Dirichlet should be strictly positive.

So the last problem we need to solve is choosing a value for α and β. One common choice is to take 1 for all of them. In terms of Dirichlet distributions, it means we choose a uniform prior for all the parameters of the class and feature variables. It means we will allow our parameters to take any value with equal probability except of course 0. Choosing different values for α and β will lead to different form results. We can try to promote certain values by pushing the Dirichlet distribution in one direction or another; or, on the contrary, we can try to keep all parameters with similar values.

If you choose 1 for the Dirichlet parameter, you will obtain something called Laplace smoothing, which we saw before in the `naiveBayes` function of the `e1071` R package. Sometimes, it is also called a pseudo-count because it could be seen as artificially adding one example of any case to your dataset.

But the Dirichlet prior is not the only possible prior we can use. In the case of binary variables, another distribution of interest is the Beta distribution. In the next section we will present more formally the Beta-Binomial model and see its relation to the Dirichlet-Multinomial model we just saw. We will see that the results are similar and also how to play with the parameters of the Beta distribution in order to describe different types of prior for our class and feature variables.

Beta-Binomial

The Beta-Binomial prior is another example and a well-known model where we set a prior distribution on the parameter of the distribution of interest. Here we are going to use a binomial distribution with a θ parameter. The θ parameter can be seen as a probability that an event will occur or not, or a proportion of the positive events in a sequence of experiments. Therefore, the parameter θ takes values in $[0,1]$.

Let's first review the Binomial distribution with a simple example: let's say we have a coin and we want to know if the coin is impartial or not when we play the heads or tails game. The game is to toss the coin N times and try to estimate what is the probability θ of obtaining a head. This problem is very important because it is the basis of many other models. You can replace the game of heads or tails with the result of experimentation (positive or negative), the result of a poll (yes or no), or any other binary answer.

Historically, this model has been studied by Thomas Bayes and generalized by Laplace, thus giving birth to the Bayes rule (or more formally the Bayes-Laplace, as we saw in *Chapter 1, Probabilistic Reasoning*).

In this problem we will follow again a Bayesian approach: we need a **prior distribution** on the parameter θ, a **likelihood of the data given the parameter** $p(x \mid \theta)$, and we will compute the **posterior distribution** $p(\theta \mid x)$.

If we want to be complete, we can also compute the predictive posterior distribution $p(x \mid \theta, x)$, which is the distribution of a new data point (a new toss) given parameters and the previous experiments.

When we assume that all the observations (that is, the results of each toss) are independently and identically distributed we can again write that:

$$p(D \mid \theta) = \prod_{i=1}^{N} p(x_i \mid \theta)$$

Here, $D = \{x_1, \ldots, x_N\}$ is the dataset.

Is this assumption true? From a theoretical point of view, it's true because: (1) every time we toss a coin, the previous toss has no influence on the new one and (2) we use the same coin for all the tosses, so the parameter θ doesn't change. Therefore the distribution of heads and tails is the same. But is it true in real life? If we assume that each toss can microscopically change the air in the room and that each toss will rip off a few atoms of metal from the coin, then the distribution is certainly not independent and certainly not identical. But in fact the acute reader will have understood that those effects are so negligible that they have absolutely no influence on the results. Maybe one should toss the coin a few billion times to start seeing a difference.

However, when designing such an experiment, one has to be careful about the conditions of the experimentation and be sure that the data is indeed identically and independently distributed. For example, if the experiment is a poll and one puts the same question to people next to each other, one after the other, it is very likely that the second person will be influenced by the answer of the first one. And therefore the data will not be *iid* anymore.

Now we can star solving our Bayesian problem by assuming distributions for all the required components.

The Bernoulli distribution is a probability distribution that gives the probability θ to a random variable when it takes the value 1 and $(1-\theta)$ if it takes the value 0. We say that $x \sim Ber(\theta)$, that is $p(x \mid \theta) = \theta^x (1-\theta)^{1-x}$ with $x \in \{0,1\}$. If we repeat the same Bernoulli experiment many times (that is, if we toss the coin many times), we obtain the dataset $D = \{x_1, \ldots, x_N\}$ with this probability distribution:

$$p(D \mid \theta) = \prod_{i=1}^{N} p(x_i \mid \theta) = \theta^{x_1} (1-\theta)^{1-x_1} \theta^{x_2} (1-\theta)^{1-x_2} \ldots \theta^{x_N} (1-\theta)^{1-x_N}$$

Because of the *iid* assumption and the fact that the product is commutative, and if we call N_1 the number of heads and N_0 the number of tails, we can rewrite this likelihood by:

$$p(D \mid \theta) = \theta^{N_1} (1-\theta)^{N_0}$$

From now on, we can take the log of this expression:

$$LL(\theta) = \log \theta^{N_1} (1-\theta)^{N_0} = N_1 \log \theta + N_0 \log (1-\theta)$$

Before going further, it's interesting to understand why we are always using logarithms in our computations. The first reason is historical: probabilities are numbers between 0 and 1. Multiplying two probabilities is essential when computing the likelihood of iid data. In fact, in such a likelihood, it's not unusual to multiply hundreds or thousands of those probabilities. On early computers, multiplication was very slow compared to addition. Because $\log(a.b) = \log(a) + \log(b)$, it was useful to first transform all the data into logarithms and then add them. It was generally faster. Nowadays, this is not true anymore and usually multiplication can be (almost) as fast as addition. The cost of computing the logarithm can sometimes overwhelm the small gain of just doing additions instead of multiplications.

The second reason is that, when we multiply numbers between 0 and 1, the result tends to decrease and be smaller and smaller. This time, even modern computers have a limited capacity to represent numbers and moreover, because real values are discretized (usually following the IEEE-754 norm), the accuracy of computations suffers enormously and errors are accumulated throughout the computations, leading to very inaccurate if not false results. However, with logarithms, numbers between $-\infty$ and 0 are added together, making the computations more accurate. Small values are now contributing a lot to the results, making computations accurate.

Usually we take the negative log-likelihood, and we only have to deal with positive numbers. The other reason is that, when one wants to maximize the likelihood, one can also minimize (towards zero) the negative log-likelihood. This is an equivalent problem. And a lot of optimization algorithms try to find the zeros of functions. Therefore implementation is simpler.

To illustrate this, just plot the following in R:

```
x <- seq(0,1,0.05)
plot(x, -log(x), t='b', col=1)
```

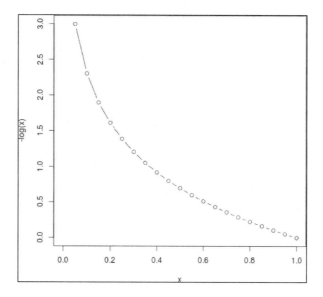

After this parenthesis, we are back to the problem of a sequence of tosses. So we assumed that the random variable representing the result of a toss has a Bernoulli distribution and we calculated the likelihood of a sequence of N tosses.

Now let's consider the problem from a different angle and let's assume we toss the coin N times, N being known in advance. The question is now: what is the probability of obtaining N_1 heads out of N tosses.

On average, the answer will depend on how the coin is biased. And the bias of the coin is known too; it is the parameter θ. If $\theta = 0.5$, then N_1 should rather be $\frac{N}{2}$. We want to have a probability for each possible value that could take N_1 in the function of θ and N. In this case, it is important to remark the following: how many positive cases do we have? By positive cases, we mean, How many sequences of N tosses can provide N_1 heads? On a small example with $N=3$ and $N_1=2$, we can have *{HHT, HTH, THH}*. That is three possibilities. In general, we want to know the number of combinations of r values out of n events with replacement. And this is equal to $\binom{n}{r} = \frac{n!}{r!(n-r)!}$. Now remember that each sequence is independent of the others and that the probability of two independent events is the sum of probability $P(A \lor B) = P(A) + P(B)$. So finally, the probability of $N_1 = \binom{n}{r}$ independent Bernoulli events of parameter θ is:

$$p(N_1 \mid \theta, N_0) = \binom{N_1 + N_0}{N_1} \theta^{N_1} (1-\theta)^{N_0}$$

This probability distribution is very well-known and is called the **Binomial distribution**. In fact, the Binomial distribution is usually defined with two parameters: N, the total number of tosses, and θ. It is commonly written as:

$$p(n \mid \theta, N) = \binom{N}{n} \theta^n (1-\theta)^{N-n}$$

In R, the binomial distribution is provided by default in the language and it can be used with the following functions:

- `dbinom`: Density
- `pbinom`: Cumulative
- `qbinom`: Quantile
- `rbinom`: Random generation

We can illustrate the distribution of the binomial in R with the little program that follows:

```
x<-seq(1,20)
plot(x,dbinom(x,20,0.5),t='b',col=1,ylim=c(0,0.3))
```

```
lines(x,dbinom(x,20,0.3),t='b',col=2)
lines(x,dbinom(x,20,0.1),t='b',col=3)
```

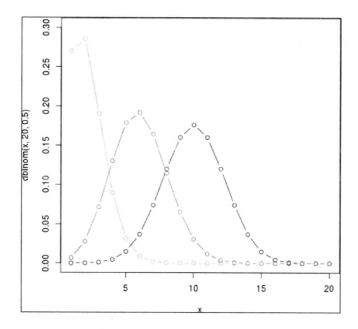

We show three different distributions with the parameter θ varying from 0.1 to 0.5. When θ is small, obviously the probability of having many positive outcomes quickly decreases. When θ is 0.5, the black curve shows that the probability of 50% positive outcomes is obviously the highest.

The prior distribution

The next question that arises is, What prior distribution should we use as a prior on θ? The beta distribution is a very common choice and has the nice property of being a conjugate to the Binomial and Bernoulli distributions.

In fact the beta distribution has a very nice form, similar to the Binomial and Bernoulli distributions, as follows:

$$p(\theta \mid \alpha, \beta) \propto \theta^{\alpha-1} (1-\theta)^{\beta-1}$$

We will add the normalization constant later. The good thing about the Beta is that its domain, that is, the value that θ can take, is [0,1]. And therefore θ from the Beta distribution can also be interpreted as a proportion or a probability and used as a parameter in the Binomial or Bernoulli distributions. This makes the Beta distribution a perfect candidate for the prior distribution. To complete the formula we have to realize that this distribution is a density and the integral over its domain must be one. Therefore it is usual to write:

$$p(\theta \mid \alpha, \beta) = \frac{\theta^{\alpha-1}(1-\theta)^{\beta-1}}{\int_0^1 x^{\alpha-1}(1-x)^{\beta-1}\, dx}$$

And the integral at the denominator is known as the Beta function. In general we can simply write the density as:

$$p(\theta \mid \alpha, \beta) = \frac{1}{Beta(\alpha, \beta)}\theta^{\alpha-1}(1-\theta)^{\beta-1} = \frac{\Gamma(\alpha+\beta)}{\Gamma(\alpha)\Gamma(\beta)}\theta^{\alpha-1}(1-\theta)^{\beta-1}$$

Here, the Gamma function is defined as:

$$\Gamma(x) = \int_0^\infty \exp(-t)t^{x-1}\, dt$$

When x is an integer $\Gamma(x) = (c-1)!$

The posterior distribution with the conjugacy property

Now we need to combine the Binomial distribution with the Beta prior to obtain the posterior distribution. The posterior distribution is obtained by applying the Bayes rule as usual:

$$p(\theta \mid N, n, \alpha, \beta) = \frac{p(n \mid N, \theta)\, p(\theta \mid N, \alpha, \beta)}{p(n \mid N, \alpha, \beta)} \propto p(n \mid N, \theta)\, p(\theta \mid N, \alpha, \beta)$$

And finally, by replacing each distribution with its analytical form, we obtain:

$$p(n \mid N, \theta) p(\theta \mid N, \alpha, \beta) = \frac{N!}{n!(N-n)!} \theta^n (1-\theta)^{N-n} \times \frac{\Gamma(\alpha)\Gamma(\beta)}{\Gamma(\alpha+\beta)} \theta^{\alpha-1} (1-\theta)^{\beta-1}$$

And this is simply proportional to:

$$\theta^n (1-\theta)^{N-n} \times \theta^{\alpha-1} (1-\theta)^{\beta-1} = \theta^{n+\alpha-1} (1-\theta)^{N-n+\beta-1}$$

And in fact the last form is exactly the same as the initial form of the Beta distribution. It means that our posterior distribution on θ is also Beta-distributed.

Therefore, we have found our posterior and we can resume this calculus as follows:

If n follows a Binomial distribution *Binomial(θ, N)* and the prior distribution over θ is *Beta(a, β)*, then the posterior distribution on θ will also be a Beta distribution *Beta(α + n, β+ N – n)*.

In this case, thanks to the conjugacy property, we've made a very efficient posterior computation, which boils down to a few additions only. The notion of conjugacy is extremely important in Bayesian reasoning mainly for this property.

Which values should we choose for the Beta parameters?

This will depend on what type of information we want to include in the model. For example, we might decide that every value of θ is *a priori* acceptable and we want to give the same importance to all of them. This is what we did with the Dirichlet distribution in the previous section when adding pseudo-counts of 1.

With the Beta distribution, we can have a uniform distribution with the parameters *Beta(1,1)*. But we can also try to give more importance to extreme values close to 0 or 1, with for example a *Beta(0.5,0.5)* distribution. On the other hand, to force θ to stay more centered around 0.5, we can use *Beta(2,2)*, *Beta(3,3)*. The higher the values, the more probability mass is given to the center. The next code in R shows different distributions with different values:

```
x <- seq(0,1,length=100)
par(mfrow=c(2,2))
```

```
param <- list(
  list(c(2,1),c(4,2),c(6,3),c(8,4)),
  list(c(2,2),c(3,2),c(4,2),c(5,2)),
  list(c(1,1),c(2,2),c(3,3),c(4,4)),
  list(c(0.5,0.5),c(0.5,1),c(0.8,0.8)))
for(p in param)
{
  c <- 1
  leg <- character(0)
  fill <- integer(0)
  plot(0,0,type='n', xlim=c(0,1),ylim=c(0,4))
  for(v in p)
  {
    lines(x,dbeta(x,v[1],v[2]),col=c)
    leg <- c(leg, paste0("Beta(",v[1],",",v[2],")"))
    fill <- c(fill,c)
    c <- c+1
  }
  legend(0.65,4,leg,fill,bty="n") }
```

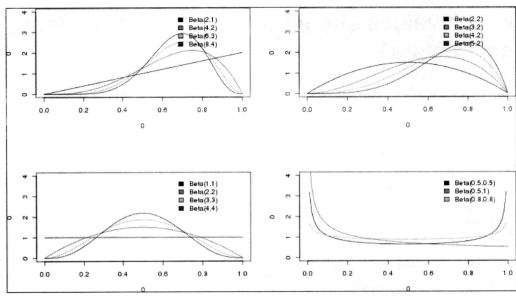

The Gaussian mixture model

The Gaussian mixture model is the first example of a latent variable model. Latent variables are also called hidden variables and are variables that are present in the model but are never observed.

The notion of using unobserved variables can be surprising at first because we might wonder how to estimate the parameters of the distribution of such a variable. In fact, we might wonder what the real meaning of such a latent variable is.

For example, let's say we observe data represented by a group of random variables. This data tends to group into clusters, aggregating together depending on their underlying meaning. For example, we could observe physiological traits from animals and group those data points by species such as dogs, cats, cows, and so on. If we think in terms of generating models, then we can say that, by choosing a group such as for example pony, we will observe features that are specific to this group and not to another group such as cats. However, none of the physiological variables carry an explicit reference to the fact that they come from the pony group or the cat group.

This distinction only exists because we want to group things together but they're not part of the real world. However, it helps a lot to group data like this, by pony or cat features, to understand animals in general. This is the grouping we want to do with a latent variable.

Using latent variables in a model can be problematic at first because there is no data to estimate their distribution. However, we saw before that algorithms such as EM can be very helpful when it comes to solving this task.

Moreover, we can simplify the model by introducing some conditional independence between features or a hierarchy between variables, thus making the model easier to interpret or easier to compute.

The Gaussian mixture model is a latent variable mainly used for density estimation problems, where, roughly speaking, the main assumption is that a random process will, according to a multinomial distribution, choose a Gaussian at random and then (according to this selected Gaussian distribution) choose a data point at random. It is a very simple 2-step process. And it also simplifies the problem of estimating a complex dataset distribution. Instead of searching for a very complex distribution, the model estimates it with a set of simple Gaussian distributions, joined by the latent variable. It is similar to a divide-and-conquer approach.

Definition

In this model we will call X the variable we can observe and we will call Z a multinomial random variable that is hidden. The model is defined by the following probability distribution:

$$p(X \mid \Theta) = \sum_i p(Z_i = 1 \mid \pi_i) p(X \mid Z_i = 1, \theta_i)$$
$$= \sum_i \pi_i p(X \mid Z_i = 1, \theta_i)$$

Here, π_i are the **mixing proportions** and $p(X \mid Z_i = 1, \theta_i)$ are the **mixture components**. In this formula, because Z is a multinomial distribution, we have $p(Z_i \mid \pi_i) = \pi_i$ and Z_i is the ith component of Z.

Finally Θ is the set of all parameters of the model and θ_i are the parameters of the X variables.

When X has a Gaussian distribution, we can write the preceding distribution as:

$$p(X \mid \Theta) = \sum_i \pi_i N\left(X \mid \theta_i = (\mu_i, \Sigma_i)\right)$$

Here, Σ_i are the covariance matrices of the variable X. If we expand the formula we obtain:

$$p(X \mid \Theta) = \sum_i \pi_i \frac{1}{(2\pi)^{m/2} |\Sigma_i|^{1/2}} \exp\left(-\frac{1}{2}(x - \mu_i)^T \Sigma_i^{-1}(x - \mu_i)\right)$$

This result looks dense but it's time to draw the corresponding probabilistic graphical model and see the equivalence in it:

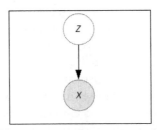

This represents the probability distribution $P(X,Z)$ where, this time, the Z node is white to indicate that it is hidden or latent. If we marginalize out the variable Z from this model to obtain the distribution on X we will obtain exactly the previous formula. Also note that, in this model, X has a multivariate Gaussian distribution.

From this distribution it is also simple to compute the posterior of Z given X. This is a value of interest: we want to know what the probability is of Z being in state i after observing Z; in other words, it gives us information about which distribution the observed variable comes from. Indeed, let's first draw a mixture of three Gaussians in R with the following code. This time we will use the package called `mixtools`:

```
N <- 400

X <- list(
  mvrnorm(N, c(1,1), matrix(c(1,-0.5,-0.5,1),2,2)/4),
  mvrnorm(N, c(3,3), matrix(c(2,0.5,0.5,1),2,2)/4),
  mvrnorm(N, c(5,5), matrix(c(1,-0.5,-0.5,4),2,2)/4))

plot(0,0,xlim=c(-1,7),ylim=c(-1,7),type='n')

for(i in 1:3)
  points(X[[i]],pch=18+i, col=1+i)
```

This little program simply generates three sets of data from a multivariate Gaussian distribution with two dimensions. It plots the three datasets on the same graph and as expected the points create three clusters of data, as shown in the next figure. If we regroup the three little datasets into a big one, one interesting problem would be to find out the parameters of the three clusters. In this example, we have an ideal situation because we generated an equal number of points for each cluster. But in real applications, this will rarely be the case.

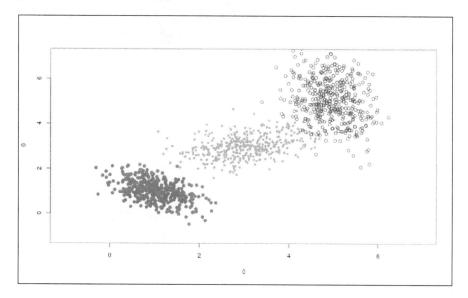

The posterior probability of the hidden variable Z can be written as

$$p(Z_i = 1 | X, \Theta) = \frac{p(X | Z_i = 1, \theta_i) p(Z_i = 1 | \pi_i)}{p(X | \Theta)}$$

$$= \frac{\pi_i N(X, \mu_i | \Sigma_i)}{\sum_j \pi_j N(X, \mu_j | \Sigma_j)}$$

This is a simple application of the Bayes rule again.

The next step is to estimate the parameters θ of the model, assuming again that the data is *iid*. If we call $D = \{x_n\}$ the dataset, we can, as before, write the log-likelihood of the model:

$$LL(\Theta | D) = \sum_n \log p(x_n | \Theta)$$

$$= \sum_n \log \left\{ \sum_i \pi_i N(x_n | \mu_i, \Sigma_i) \right\}$$

This log-likelihood is a bit hard to optimize and we will use an adequate optimization algorithm. As mentioned before, the fact that a variable is hidden will lead us to use the EM algorithm.

From the previous example, we will assume that the variable Z has three states $\{z_1, z_2, z_3\}$ for each of the three Gaussian components. The only constraint in the Gaussian mixture model is that one has to assume the number of Gaussians beforehand. Other models exist where the number of Gaussian components is also a random variable and the learning algorithm will try to discover the most probable number of components while at the same time finding the mean and covariance matrix of each component.

Here we use the same code as previously:

```
library(mixtools)

N <- 400

X <- list(
    mvrnorm(N, c(1,1), matrix(c(1,-0.5,-0.5,1),2,2)/4),
    mvrnorm(N, c(3,3), matrix(c(2,0.5,0.5,1),2,2)/4),
    mvrnorm(N, c(5,5), matrix(c(1,-0.5,-0.5,4),2,2)/4))
x <- do.call(rbind,X) # transform X into a matrix
model2 <-  mvnormalmixEM(x, verb=TRUE)
model3 <- mvnormalmixEM(x, k=3,verb=TRUE)
```

It will take some time to compute the results. The parameter `verb=TRUE` displays the result of each iteration of the EM algorithm. What is interesting to see is the log-likelihood. In the first case (`model2`), the log-likelihood will go from approximately 3711 to -3684 in 27 steps. Your results might be different because remember that we generate the dataset at random using `mvrnorm`.

The problem with `model2` is that the number of components is taken by default to be 2: you can perform `help(mvnormalmixEM)` in R to see the parameter `k`. And we know we have three components in this mixture. However, `model3` has a number of components `k=3`, closer to the real dataset, and obviously the log-likelihood will be closer to 3. It goes from 3,996 to only 3,305 in 41 iterations (again it might be slightly different on your computer). So it seems the convergence has been far better in the second case when we assume the correct number of components.

We can now plot the log-likelihood evolution of the EM algorithm to understand the difference between the two models:

```
plot(model2,xlim=c(0,50),ylim=c(-4000,-3000))
par(new=T)
plot(model,lt=3,xlim=c(0,50),ylim=c(-4000,-3000))
```

Note that, by fixing the size of the graph, we can easily superimpose the two graphs. The dashed line is the graph corresponding to the model with three components. It is clear that the log-likelihood gets closer to zero during this algorithm. However, it takes more iterations to reach this result.

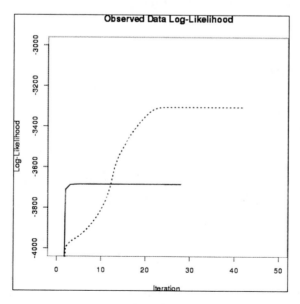

By looking at the results in `model3`, we can have a better understanding of the model that has been found by the EM algorithm:

```
model3$lambda
```

```
[1] 0.3358283 0.3342840 0.3298877
```

The proportions of each component are, as expected, very close to our initial proportions. You can change the number of points for each component and check again:

```
X <- list(
    mvrnorm(100, c(1,1), matrix(c(1,-0.5,-0.5,1),2,2)/4),
    mvrnorm(200, c(3,3), matrix(c(2,0.5,0.5,1),2,2)/4),
    mvrnorm(300, c(5,5), matrix(c(1,-0.5,-0.5,4),2,2)/4))
x <- do.call(rbind,X)
```

And then let's rerun it with `mixtools`:

```
model3.2 <- mvnormalmixEM(x, k=3,verb=TRUE)
```

We can see the log-likelihood going from approximately -1925 to -1691 in 84 iterations. But now the proportions are 0.3378457, 0.1651263, and 0.4970280 which indeed correspond to the proportions we initially set in our toy dataset.

Again we can check the other parameters, and see they are similar to those we set up in our dataset. In a real-world application, we don't have any idea of the location and covariance of each component, of course. But this example shows that the EM algorithm usually converges to the desired values:

```
model3$mu
[[1]]
[1] 3.025684 3.031763
[[2]]
[1] 0.9854002 1.0289426
[[3]]
[1] 4.989129 5.076438
```

Now it's time to look at the result more graphically to really understand which components have been found by the EM algorithm.

First of all, we plot `model3` with the following command and display its three components with `plot(model3, which=2)`:

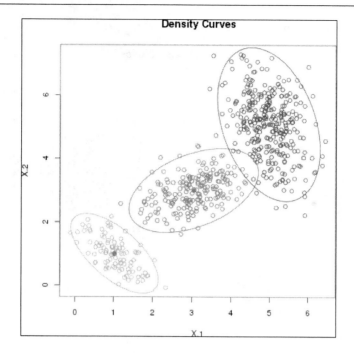

Then we display, for comparison purposes, `model2` and `model3.2`:

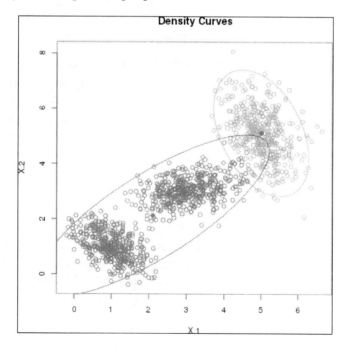

The following figure shows `model3.2`:

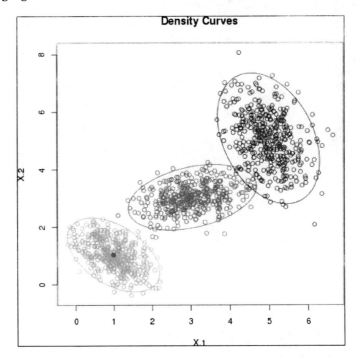

And now we conclude from our observations:

- `model3` and `model3.2` are extremely similar, as expected.
- `model2`, for which we chose to have only two components, seems to have made an acceptable choice with the components. Indeed the two bottom components have an almost similar orientation. So the algorithm converged toward a solution in which one Gaussian will embed the two bottom components, and another Gaussian will embed the top one, which has a different orientation. It is a good result.

Summary

In this chapter we used the simple yet powerful Bayesian model, which has a representation as a probabilistic graphical model. We saw a Bayesian treatment of the over-fitting problem with the use of priors, such as the Dirichlet-multinomial and the famous Beta-Binomial model.

The last section introduced another graphical model, which was around before the invention of probabilistic graphical models and is called the Gaussian mixture. It is a very important model to capture data coming from different subsets within the same model. And finally, we saw another application of the EM algorithm: learning such models and finding out the parameters of each Gaussian component.

Of course, the Gaussian mixture is not the only latent variable model; in fact it represents a lot of Bayesian models and the probabilistic graphical model framework.

In the next chapter, we will continue our study of inference algorithms for Bayesian models and probabilistic graphical models with the introduction of a new and very important family of algorithms: the sampling algorithm, also known as the Monte-Carlo algorithm. It is arguably one of the most important algorithms in the field of machine learning because it allows the use of many types of model that were previously too complicated to use.

5

Approximate Inference

This chapter introduces a second class of inference algorithms, maybe the most important of all because of their versatility. The approach is completely different from what we have seen until now. Indeed, we saw two classes of algorithms, one based on a pure analytic resolution of the problem by calculating manually the posterior distribution and the other one by using message propagation in a graph. In both cases, the result was computed exactly. In the case of an analytic solution, computing the solution usually boils down to computing a function of the posterior distribution. In the case of a message-passing algorithm, computing the posterior distribution is done step-by-step by propagating messages on a graph. If the graph is not appropriate for this type of algorithm, the computations can be extremely long and often intractable.

However, in many cases, we can trade a bit of accuracy for more speed. This is the main idea of approximate inference. Does it really matter if we are less accurate? Well, it appears that, in many applications, approximate inference is still very accurate. On the other hand, it allows us to deal with more complex models and with many types of distributions, something that is not completely possible with the other approaches.

In this chapter, we will see one important class of algorithms, called **sampling algorithms**, also known as **Monte-Carlo sampling**. The main idea of this class of algorithms is to draw at random from the posterior distribution in order to replace complex computations with simple statistics. For example, if we want to compute the posterior mean of a random variable, we can draw many samples at random from its posterior distribution and simply compute the mean of the values we obtained.

Monte-Carlo sampling is what really made the Bayesian revolution possible in science. Before, Bayesian models were hard to compute, if not impossible.

More specifically, we will look at the following algorithms:

- Rejection and importance sampling, as a basis for many other methods
- Markov Chain Monte-Carlo and the Metropolis-Hastings algorithm

These two classes of algorithms will cover most of what we need to know about the Monte-Carlo method. However, many new algorithms are regularly being discovered.

Sampling from a distribution

We have a big problem with probabilistic graphical models in general: they are intractable. They quickly become so complex that it is impossible to run anything in a reasonable amount of time. Not to mention learning them. Remember, for a simple algorithm such as EM, we need to compute a posterior distribution at each iteration. If the dataset is big, which is common now, if the model has a lot of dimensions, which is also common, it becomes totally prohibitive. Moreover, we limited ourselves to a small class of distributions, such as multinomial or Gaussian distributions. Even if they can cover a wide range of applications, it's not the case all the time.

In this chapter, we consider a new class of algorithms based on the idea of sampling from a distribution. Sampling here means to draw values of the parameters at random, following a particular distribution. For example, if one throws a dice, one draws a sample from a multinomial distribution, such that six values are possible, with equal probability. The result is a number between 1 and 6. If the die is not fair (say 6 has a higher probability), then it is possible we will obtain more 6s than the other numbers. If we throw the die many times and then calculate the mean value of all the results, we will presumably see a number closer to 6 than 3.

In many situations, we are more interested in some properties of the distribution rather than the distribution itself—for example, its mean or variance. It means that, in many cases, we want to compute an expectation of a function $f(x)$ with respect to a probability distribution $p(x)$. Here, x can be any random variable of any dimension we want. For example, $p(x)$ can be a multivariate Gaussian distribution or a probabilistic graphical model.

In the case of continuous variables, we want to solve the generic problem of evaluating the expectation:

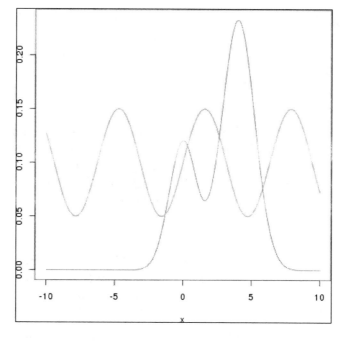

$$E(f) = \int f(x)p(x)dx$$

When x is discrete, the integral is replaced by a summation.

In the example in the screenshot, the distribution is in red and the function in green. We immediately see there will be many problems sampling from such a complex distribution.

The algorithms presented in this chapter will try to solve many of those problems.

The main idea in sampling is to replace the evaluation of an integral with a simpler sum over a set of samples drawn independently from the distribution $p(x)$. The previous expectation can then be approximated by a finite sum:

$$\hat{f} = \frac{1}{L}\sum_{l=1}^{L} f\left(x^{(l)}\right)$$

If the samples are drawn from the distribution $p(x)$ then $E(\hat{f}) = E(f)$ and, similarly, the variance of the estimator is:

$$var(\hat{f}) = \frac{1}{L} E\left(f - E(f)^2\right)$$

In this method, the problem is to obtain independent samples. It is not always the case and the number of effective samples might be fewer than the number of points drawn from the distribution. However, as seen in the previous formula, the variance of $\hat{f}$, the estimator does not depend on the dimension of x. It means that, even in high-dimensional problem such as a graphical model, high accuracy can be obtained with a relatively small number of samples.

But as we stated before, the main problem is in particular sampling from the distribution $p(x)$. And it can be hard or even impossible to do it sometimes. When the distribution $p(x)$ is a graphical model in a directed form (such as most of the models we have in this book), the technique to draw a sample is quite simple and called **ancestral sampling**.

Given an ordering of the variables x_i in the graph, from the top of the graph to the bottom, one can draw a sample from the graphical model by sampling successively each variable and then assigning the sampled values at the corresponding variables to sample from its descendant. For example, let's say we have the following graph:

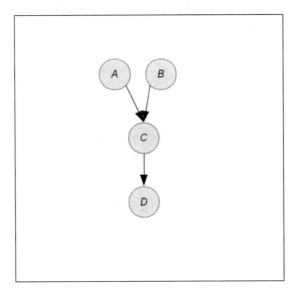

We start by sampling from *p(A)* and *p(B)* independently, then assign the sampled values to *A=a* and *B=b* so that we sample from *p(C | A=a, B=b)*. Finally, the last sample is drawn from *p(D | C=c)*. If none of the variables are observed, the procedure is very simple. If, however, one variable is observed, one technique is to keep only the samples that agree with the value of the observed variables. If we have *A=a1*, for example, then we will keep only the samples in which we have been lucky enough to have *A=a1*. In this case, not all the samples are usable and the difference between the number of drawn samples and the number of useful samples can be big, because each time a set of samples disagrees with the observed values, it has to be discarded. The probability of a set of samples being accepted decreases with the number of observed nodes.

Basic sampling algorithms

We start our study of sampling algorithms by looking at some basic algorithms that can be used as subroutines in more advanced schemes. In all the algorithms from this book, we assume that we can generate random numbers uniformly from the interval [0,1]. The problem of generating random numbers on a computer is complex and vast. In most cases, random numbers will be generated by a deterministic algorithm, and they are called **pseudo-random numbers**. They are not random, but their distribution and properties are close enough to a real random generator that they can be used as real random numbers. Pseudo-random number generators are usually based on the estimation of chaotic functions that are extremely sensitive to their initial conditions, which are called the **seed**. Changing the value can generate a completely different sequence of numbers, even if the seed value is just a little bit different from the previous one. Nowadays, we also have electronic devices that can generate random numbers from physical phenomena such as thermal noise, photoelectric effects, or quantum phenomena.

Standard distributions

In R, it is possible to generate random numbers from standard distributions. However, for the sake of understanding, we will review simple techniques for how to generate random numbers from a uniform distribution only.

In R, random numbers can be generated from a family of functions beginning with the letter r, such as `runif`, `rnorm`, `rbeta`, `rbinom`, `rcauchy`, `rgamma`, `rgeom`, `rhyper`, `rlogis`, and so on. In fact, density can be estimated using the functions beginning with d, and the cumulative distribution function with functions beginning with the letter p.

For example:

```
runif(1)
```

```
[1] 0.593396
```

Here, the parameter of the function is the number of numbers one wants:

```
runif(10)
```

```
 [1] 0.7334754 0.2519494 0.7332522 0.9194623 0.5867712 0.3880692 0.2869559
 [8] 0.7379801 0.4886681 0.5329107
```

Of course, these are (pseudo) random numbers, so your results will be different from the examples shown earlier.

```
rnorm(1,10,1)
```

```
[1] 9.319718
```

This generates a normally distributed number, with mean 10 and variance 1. If we generate many of these numbers and plot the running mean, we'll see the mean converging little by little to its true value. This is the main property we will use throughout this chapter and in sampling algorithms in general.

```
x<-rnorm(1000,10,1)
y<-cumsum(x)/(1:1000)
plot(y,t='l')
abline(h=10)
```

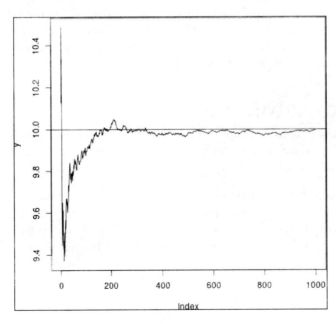

Generating a random number from a simple distribution is the basis of all sampling algorithms. Here, we consider we know how to generate a random number from a uniform distribution. In R, we perform `runif(1,0,1)`. By default, the min and max parameters are already 0 and 1. Therefore `runif(1)` will do.

Suppose we transform the uniformly random values with a function $f(.)$ such that $y=f(x)$. The distribution of y will be:

$$p(y) = p(x)\left|\frac{dx}{dy}\right|$$

We need functions $f(x)$ such that the distributions of y are distributed according to the desired distribution $p(y)$. Integrating $p(y)$, we have:

$$x = h(y) \equiv \int_{-\infty}^{y} p(\hat{y})d\hat{y}$$

Therefore, $y = h^{-1}(x)$, which is the inverse function on the indefinite integral of the desired distribution. Let's take a simple example with the exponential distribution. This distribution is continuous with a density function $p(x) = \lambda \exp(-\lambda x)$ and a support on [0, +∞[. Integrating $h(y)$ gives $h(y) = 1 - \exp(-\lambda y)$, which is the cumulative distribution function of the exponential distribution.

As a side note, the exponential distribution is useful to describe the lengths of inter-arrival times in a Poisson process. It can be viewed as the continuous version of the geometric distribution.

Therefore, if we transform our uniformly distributed variable x with the function $h^{-1} = -\lambda^{-1} \ln(1-x)$, then y will be exponentially distributed.

We can check it experimentally by plotting the distribution of our function and comparing it with the distribution of an exponential distribution. We take `lambda=2` in this example:

```
x<-runif(20000)
inv_h<-function(x,lambda) -(1/lambda)*log(1-x)
hist(inv_h(x,2),breaks=100,freq=F)
t<-seq(0,4,0.01)
lines(t,dexp(t,2),lw=2)
```

We first generate 20,000 points from a uniform U(0,1) distribution. Then, `inv_h` is the function defined earlier and we plot a histogram. Note the parameter `freq=F` to draw with the densities instead of the frequency. Finally, we draw the density function of an exponential distribution with the same parameter (the thick black line in the following graph) and see that the two distributions, the empirical one and the analytic one, are a very good match.

The following screenshot shows the result:

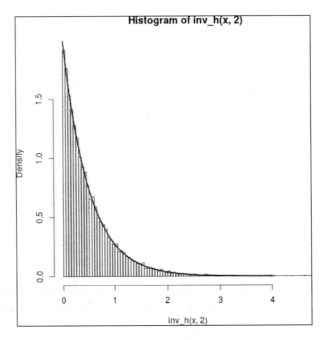

The problem with this technique is the evaluation of the indefinite integral. In simple cases, this integral is readily available but this is not always so. In such a case, we need another strategy and the key is to use a simpler distribution to approximate the more complex distribution we can sample from. There are two basic techniques to do that. One is called **rejection sampling,** and it uses a simple distribution to draw a sample from and accept the sample at the same time as it falls into the more complex distribution. Otherwise it is rejected. The other technique is called **importance sampling** and, in this case, samples from the approximate distribution are corrected to take into account their difference with respect to the original distribution one wants to sample from.

Both techniques are important and used as a basis for more advanced techniques, such as **Markov Chain Monte-Carlo** (MCMC), that we will see in the second part of this chapter.

In all cases, one of the main ideas is to use a **proposal distribution**, whose goal is to approximate, even roughly, the distribution we want to sample from. We will call $q(x)$ the proposal distribution and *p(x)* the initial distribution in the following sections.

Rejection sampling

Suppose we want to sample from a distribution that is not a simple one. Let's call this distribution $p(x)$ and let's assume we can evaluate $p(x)$ for any given value x, up to a normalizing constant Z, that is:

$$p(x) = \frac{1}{Z_p} \tilde{p}(x)$$

In this context, $p(x)$ is too complex to sample from but we have another simpler distribution $q(x)$ from which we can draw samples. Next, we assume there exists a constant k such that $kq(x) \geq \tilde{p}(x)$ for all values of x. The function $kq(x)$ is the comparison function as shown in the following figure:

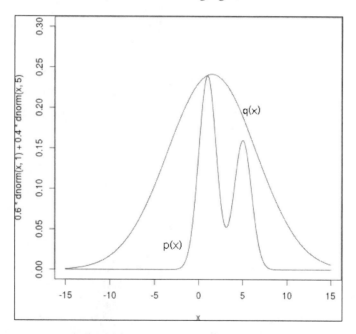

The distribution $p(x)$ has been generated with a simple plot:

```
0.6*dnorm(x,1)+0.4*dnorm(x,5)
```

The rejection sampling algorithm is based on the following idea:

- Draw a sample z_0 from $q(z)$, the proposal distribution
- Draw a second u_0 sample from a uniform distribution on $[0, kq(z_0)]$
- If $u_0 > \tilde{p}(z_0)$ then the sample is rejected otherwise u_0 is accepted

In the following figure, the pair (z_0, u_0) is rejected if it lies in the gray area. The accepted pairs are a uniform distribution under the curve of $p(z)$ and therefore the z values are distributed according to $p(z)$:

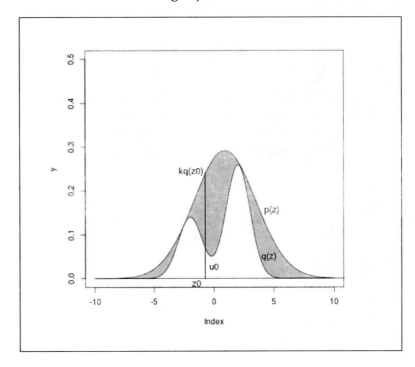

The probability of such a pair being accepted is:

$$p(accepted) = \frac{1}{k} \int \tilde{p}(z) \, dz$$

Because it depends on k, it is necessary for the proposal distribution to be as close as possible to the real distribution, otherwise the algorithm will converge very slowly and would be practically useless.

This algorithm is very simple and can be easily implemented. However, it suffers from a drastic problem related to the dimension of the problem. In the case of a probabilistic graphical model, the dimension quickly becomes very large. Rejection sampling is usually a good idea in one or two dimensions, but the rejection rate grows exponentially with the number of dimensions. However, it can be used as a subroutine in more advanced algorithms to generate samples for simple probabilistic forms (for example, at the level of one node if needed).

An implementation in R

We consider the problem of estimating a mixture of Gaussian distribution with a normal distribution. The mixture of Gaussian and the proposal distributions are shown in the following figure, where the proposal distribution in red has been scaled with *k=3.1*.

The mixture of Gaussian distribution is in black and has two modes:

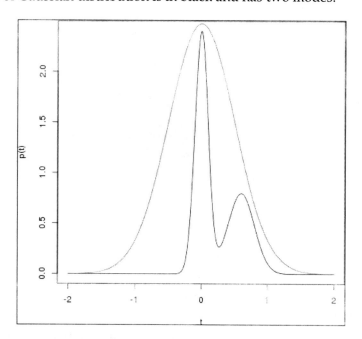

In R, we define the proposal and target distributions as follows:

```
q <- function(x) dnorm(x, 0, 0.5)
rq<- function(x) rnorm(1,  0,0.5)


p <- function(x) 0.6*dnorm(x,0,0.1)+0.4*dnorm(x,0.6,0.2)
```

The parameters are arbitrary. We have a proposal distribution q centered on 0 with a standard deviation of 0.5. The target distribution is a mixture of Gaussian with two components.

The rejection algorithm is as follows:

```
rejection <- function(N,k,p,q,rq)
{
  accept <- logical(N)
  x <- numeric(N)

  for(i in 1:N)
  {
    z0 <- rq() # draw one point from the proposal distribution
    u0 <- runif(1,0,1) # drawn one point from the uniform

    if(u0 < p(z0)/(k*q(z0))) # rejection test
      accept[i] <- TRUE
    else accept[i] <- FALSE

    x[i] <- z0
  }

  data.frame(x=x,accept=accept)
}
```

The parameters are as follows:

- N: This is the number of samples.
- k: This is the coefficient for the proposal distribution.
- p: This is the distribution to estimate. You must pass a function that takes one parameter.
- q: This is the proposal distribution (with the same remark as earlier).
- rq: This is a sampler for the proposal distribution.

This algorithm samples N times and accepts or rejects in each sample in a `for` loop. The result is stored in a `data.frame`. We keep all the samples to compare the results between rejection or not. The first column is the samples, and the second column is a binary value indicating whether the sample has been accepted or not.

The algorithm works as described in the theoretical part:

1. We first create two vectors, *accept* and *x*, for storing the results.
2. We start a loop in which:

    1. We sample *z0* from the proposal distribution.
    2. We sample *u0* from a uniform on *[0,1]*.
    3. We accept or reject the value and store the result.

Let's do a few experiments to understand the behavior of this important algorithm. In the experiments, in order for the reader to be able to reproduce exactly the same results, we will use a fixed random seed by doing:

```
set.seed(600)
```

Moreover, we will use a scaling factor k of 3.1 as:

```
k <- 3.1
```

So, the first experiment is to run the algorithm with 100 samples:

```
x <- rejection(100,k,p,q,rq)
```

The results are stored in the `data.frame` x and the head of this `data.frame` is as follows:

```
head(x)
```

	x	accept
1	-0.56007075	FALSE
2	-0.18000011	FALSE
3	-0.07572593	TRUE
4	-0.72502107	FALSE
5	-0.60916359	FALSE
6	0.97963839	FALSE

We can see that not all the points have been accepted. In our example, only 47 points out of 100 have been accepted. Looking at the histogram of the accepted values, we are far from the target distribution. It means that we need to run the algorithm longer than we did:

```
t <- seq(-2,2,0.01)
hist(x$x[x$accept],freq=F,breaks=200,col='grey')
lines(t,p(t),col=2,lwd=2)
```

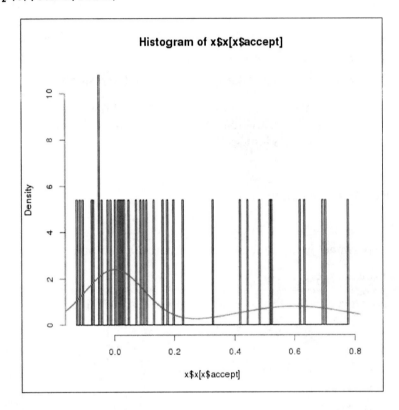

On this graph, we can see that the accepted samples regroup in the region of the high-probability mass. But running with such a small number of samples is not enough. The red curve is our target distribution.

We now run the algorithm with 5,000 samples:

```
x <- rejection(5000,k,p,q,rq)
hist(x$x[x$accept],freq=F,breaks=200,col='grey')
lines(t,p(t),col=2,lwd=2)
```

And what we expect in this second run is to see a better concentration of the accepted samples into the regions of high probability of the target distribution.

The following graph shows the result:

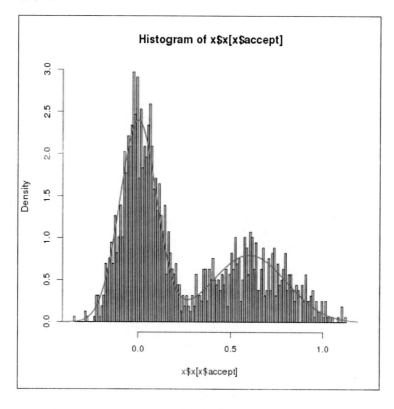

And indeed the graph looks better now. The histogram follows the true distribution but it is still not perfect. In fact, the number of accepted samples is not that high when we consider it:

```
sum(x$accept)
```

```
1581
```

If we run the algorithm for longer, we will obtain a better sample set and approach the target distribution very closely.

So, now we run the algorithm with 50,000 samples. After running it, we find that 16,158 of them have been accepted. And the result is far better of course:

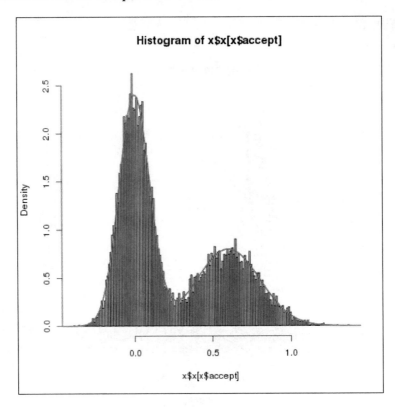

The two modes of the distribution have been correctly captured and the empirical distribution follows precisely the target distribution. This is at the expense of running the algorithm for longer.

If we draw the histogram of all the points sampled from the proposal distribution (accepted or not), they follow precisely the proposal distribution as expected:

```
hist(x$x,freq=F,breaks=200,col='grey')
lines(t,q(t),col=2,lwd=2)
```

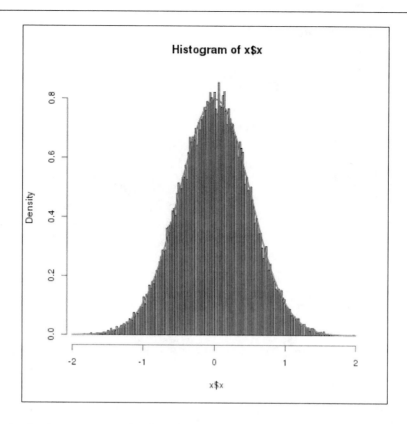

Finally, it is also interesting to look at the behavior of this algorithm from the point of view of the number of accepted samples. We run a simple function, as follows:

```
N <- sapply(seq(1000,50000,1000),
    function (n)
{
        x <- rejection(n,k,p,q,rq)
        sum(x$accept)
})
```

And we plot the result with:

```
plot(N,t='o')
```

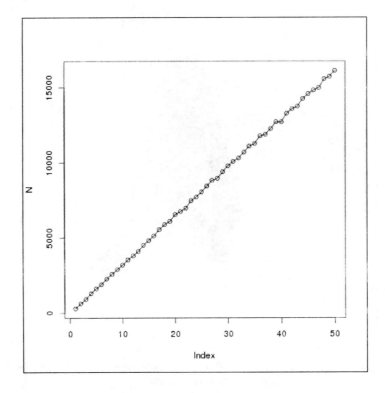

The result is not surprising. The more samples are drawn, the more are accepted, so it gives us an interesting clue: running the algorithm for longer will indeed improve the results with respect to the number of accepted samples.

But the problem with rejection sampling is that we need to sample many points in order to have good results. Rejection sampling is still a good algorithm and can be used in many situations. In the next section we will explore an improvement on rejection sampling, called **importance sampling**, in which all the sample points are accepted.

Importance sampling

Importance sampling is an improvement on rejection sampling. Again the assumptions are the same and we will use a proposal distribution $q(x)$. We also assume that we can compute the value of the density of probability $p(x)$. But we are unable to draw a sample from it because it is, again, too complex.

Importance sampling is based on the following reasoning, where we need to evaluate the expectation of a function *f(x)* with respect to the distribution *p(x)*:

$$E(f) = \int f(x)p(x)dx$$

At this stage, we simply introduce the distribution *q(x)* in the previous expression:

$$E(f) = \int f(x)\frac{p(x)}{q(x)}q(x)dx$$

And, as before, we approximate it with a finite sum:

$$\tilde{E}(f) \simeq \frac{1}{L}\sum_{l=1}^{L}\frac{p(x^{(l)})}{q(x^{(l)})}f(x^{(l)})$$

The ratio $r_l = \dfrac{p(x^{(l)})}{q(x^{(l)})}$ is called **importance weight** and it is the bias introduced by sampling *q(x)* when in fact we wanted to sample from *p(x)*. In this case, the algorithm is very simple because all the samples are used. Again, importance sampling is efficient if the proposal distribution is close enough to the original distribution. If the function *f(x)* varies a lot, we might end up in a situation where *f* has high values in areas where the distribution *p* is small and the sum might be dominated by these areas of low probability. Therefore it becomes necessary to increase the number of samples in order to have better results. So the effective number of samples might in fact be lower than the real number of samples, even if there is no rejection.

For a graphical model with discrete variables, it is possible to use importance sampling with the following approach:

- For each variable *x* in the graph:
    - If the variable is in the evidence set (*x* is observed), then set it to its own observed value.
    - Otherwise, it is sampled from *p(x | pa(x))*, in which the variables in *pa(x)* are set to their sampled (or observed) values. Therefore, sampling from *p(x | pa(x))* becomes a simple problem.

The weighting associated with the sample produced by this algorithm is:

$$r(x) = \prod_{x \in E} \frac{p(x \mid pa(x))}{p(x \mid pa(x))} \prod_{x \notin E} \frac{p(x \mid pa(x))}{1} = \prod_{x \notin E} p(x \mid pa(x))$$

The two algorithms we introduced are interesting in small dimensions and can be easily implemented. However, we saw that they suffer from severe limitations in high dimensions. Even importance sampling might need a long convergence time, despite the fact that all samples are accepted. The rest of this chapter is therefore dedicated to a very powerful and very framework based on Markov Chain and it is called **Markov Chain Monte Carlo (MCMC)**.

An implementation in R

The difference between rejection sampling and importance sampling is that the latter is not so much an algorithm to sample from a distribution as a technique to approximate averages with respect to an intractable distribution.

It is usual to use the following algorithm:

$$\int_X \frac{f(x) p(x)}{q(x)} q(x) dx \simeq \frac{\sum_{i=1}^{N} \frac{f(x_i) p(x_i)}{q(x_i)}}{\sum_{i=1}^{N} \frac{p(x_i)}{q(x_i)}}$$

Here, $x_i \sim q$, that is, x is drawn from the distribution q.

This gives us a simple algorithm because all we have to sample from q and then apply the earlier formula. We can then estimate all sorts of $f(x)$ function from this simple algorithm.

In this case, the distribution function q doesn't have to be scaled as in the rejection algorithm. Moreover, all the samples are accepted because there is no such notion as rejection. However, the algorithm is restricted to the evaluation of integrals and can't generate samples from the target distribution.

So we see that importance sampling has a different type of use case.

The algorithm can be simply implemented in R and we will use the following code:

```
importance <- function(N,f,p,q,rq)
{
  x <- sapply(1:N, rq) # sample from the proposal distribution

  A <- sum( (f(x)*p(x))/q(x) ) # numerator
  B <- sum( p(x)/q(x) ) # denominator

  return(A/B)
}
```

The parameters are as follows:

- N: This is the number of samples
- f: This is the function we want to know the expectation of
- p: This is the target distribution function
- q: This is the proposal distribution function
- rq: This is a sampler from the proposal distributions

In the following examples, we will estimate the mean of several distributions and therefore the function *f* will be the `identity` function in R.

The algorithm is very simple and follows the formula we saw before:

1. It draws *N* points from the proposal distribution.
2. It computes the numerator and denominator of the formula.
3. It returns the result.

In the next examples, we will compute the mean from the following examples:

- We will use the same mixture of Gaussian we used for rejection sampling and will approximate it with a Gaussian distribution
- We will approximate a Student's *t* distribution with a Gaussian
- We will approximate a Gamma distribution with an exponential distribution

And, as before, in order to be able to reproduce the results, we will set the seed beforehand by doing the following in R:

```
set.seed(600)
```

The first example has two distributions, where the black curve is the target distribution and the red curve is the proposal distribution. We see the same mixture of Gaussian and Gaussian as in rejection sampling:

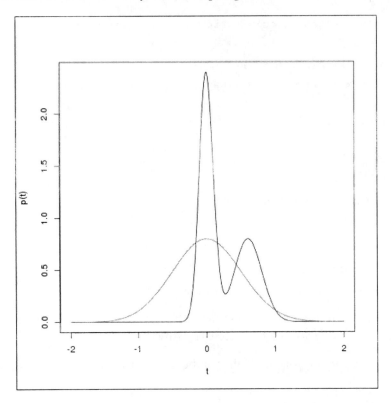

Then the next example uses a Student's t distribution and a Gaussian distribution as the proposal distribution. In this example, the Student's t distribution has 2 degrees of freedom and the Gaussian has a mean of 0 and a variance of 1.5.

The following figure shows the two distributions:

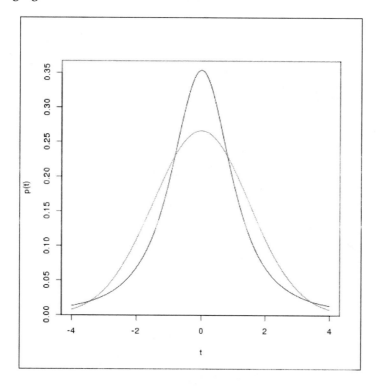

Finally, the last example uses a Gamma distribution as the target and an exponential distribution as the proposal distribution.

The shape parameter of the Gamma distribution is 2. As for the exponential distribution, the rate parameter is 0.5.

These two distributions have a support from zero to infinity. Indeed, importance sampling requires that, if the proposal distribution gives a zero probability, then the target distribution must give a zero probability too for the same value.

The following figure shows the Gamma and the exponential distribution:

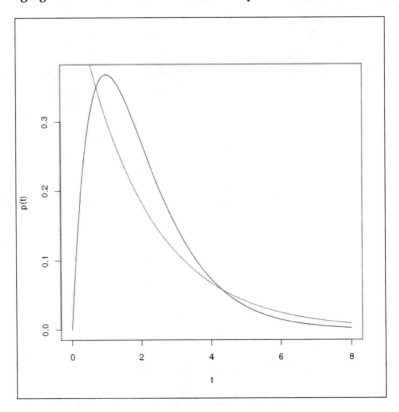

In R we define the function of our three examples as follows.

For the mixture of Gaussian approximated by a Gaussian, we have:

```
p <- function(x)  0.6*dnorm(x,0,0.1)+0.4*dnorm(x,0.6,0.2)
q <- function(x)  dnorm(x,0,0.5)
rq<- function(x)  rnorm(1,0,0.5)
```

For the Student's *t* distribution approximated by a Gaussian, we write:

```
p <- function(x)  dt(x,2)
q <- function(x)  dnorm(x,0,1.5)
rq<- function(x)  rnorm(1,0,1.5)
```

And, for the Gamma distribution approximated by an exponential function, we define:

```
p <- function(x) dgamma(x,2)
q <- function(x) dexp(x,.5)
rq<- function(x) rexp(1,.5)
```

Then we run the first experiments:

```
print(importance(1000,identity,p,q,rq))
print(importance(10000,identity,p,q,rq))
print(importance(50000,identity,p,q,rq))
```

The theoretical mean of the mixture of Gaussian is 0.24. Our code gives the following results:

```
[1] 0.2256604
[1] 0.2364267
[1] 0.2409898
```

We see that the more samples we have, the more accurate the estimation is. However, we also see that, with 10,000 samples, the result is already accurate enough. This is one of the advantages of importance sampling: we need fewer samples than rejection sampling to perform this kind of task.

The second experiment with a Student's t and a Gaussian gives the following result:

```
[1] -0.00285064
[1] 0.07353888
[1] 0.06475101
```

The theoretical result is 0 because the Student's *t* is 0-centered.

And the third experiment with a Gamma and an exponential distribution gives:

```
[1] 1.971177
[1] 2.002985
[1] 1.994183
```

Again, we see an improvement when we go from 1,000 samples to 10,000. After 10,000 samples, it seems the results are not improving a lot so we can stop the algorithm earlier.

Also note that the previous examples can be run with exactly the same lines of code as shown earlier. The reader will have to take care to the redefine the functions *p*, *q*, and *rq* each time.

The next experiment we are going to do is to run the algorithm with different sample sizes and look at how the estimated mean converges to the true value.

We will rerun the following code three times, changing the functions p, q, and rq each time:

```
t <- seq(1000,50000,500)
x <- sapply(t, function(i) importance(i, identity,p,q,rq))
```

This code iterates from 1,000 to 50,000 samples in steps of 500 on the importance sampling algorithm. The more samples we draw, the more accurate the estimated mean.

The first experiment with a mixture of Gaussian and a Gaussian gives the following result:

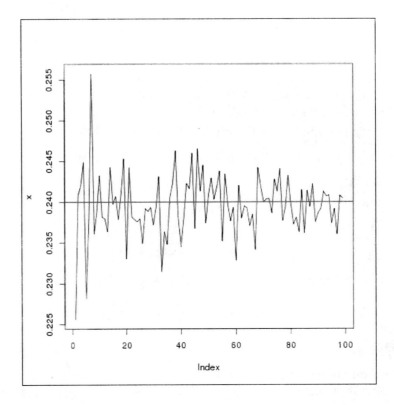

The second example with a Student's *t* distribution and a Gaussian distribution gives the following result:

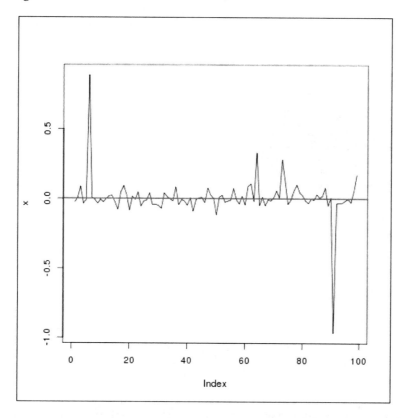

We see in this example that, despite a good convergence, we can sometimes have surprising results. It seems indeed that our proposal distribution is not the best approximation. Indeed, importance sampling can be sensitive, as with rejection sampling, to the proposal distribution and gives results that are not completely stabilized.

The last experiment uses the Gamma distribution and an exponential distribution as the proposal distribution. The following screenshot shows the result:

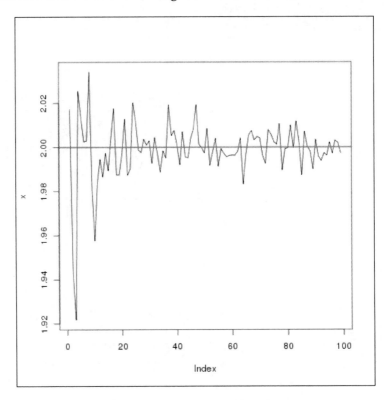

Here we see a clear convergence of the results. At the beginning, the number of samples is too low to give an accurate mean; then, when the number of samples increases, the results are more and more accurate.

In the next section, we will see a more advanced technique (to sample from arbitrary distributions) called Markov Chain Monte-Carlo sampling. It is a very powerful method and has many applications nowadays.

Markov Chain Monte-Carlo

MCMC methods have their origin in physics with the work of Metropolis, Ulam, and Rosenbluth. It was in the 1980s that they began to have a significant impact on statistics. Many MCMC algorithms and methods have been proposed and they are among the most successful approaches to computing posterior distributions.

If we use the word *framework* and not *algorithm*, it is because there is no single MCMC algorithm; instead, there are many. Multiple strategies are possible to implement it based on the problem we need to solve.

Monte-Carlo has been used for more than half a century to solve many complicated estimation problems. However, its main weakness was, as in rejection and importance sampling, its convergence in high-dimensional problems.

So Markov Chains were used from the start to estimate the convergence and stability of those methods. But it wasn't until recently (the1980s and 1990s) that they started to be massively used in statistical estimation.

General idea of the method

Markov Chain Monte-Carlo methods are based on the same idea as previously, where we have a complex distribution $p(x)$ and a proposal distribution $q(x)$. However, in this case, the state of the variable x is kept along the way and the proposal distribution depends on this current state, that is we sample from $q(x \mid x_{t-1})$. This sequence of x forms a Markov Chain.

The main idea is that at each step of the algorithm we draw a sample from $q(x \mid x_{t-1})$ and accept the sample upon certain criteria. If the sample is accepted then the parameters of q are updated according to the new sampled value and we start again, otherwise a new sample is drawn without changing q. So we want to choose a simple q distribution to make it efficient.

As before, the problem we want to solve is the expectation of a function with respect to a complex distribution:

$$E(e) = \int f(x)p(x)dx$$

We assume that we can evaluate $p(x)$ or at least we can evaluate it up to a normalizing constant $p(x) \propto \tilde{p}(x)$. In order to solve the problem of sampling, the Metropolis-Hastings algorithm (proposed by Metropolis in 1953 and Hastings in 1970) gives a generic way to construct a Markov Chain that is ergodic and stationary with respect to the distribution $p(x)$.

In other words, it means that if $x_t \sim p(x)$ then $x_{t+1} \sim p(x)$ and therefore the Markov Chain will converge to the distribution $p(x)$.

The principle of MCMC algorithms is somehow contrary to the principle of rejection and importance sampling in the sense that, instead of aiming directly at the big picture with the proposal distribution, it tries to explore the space of $p(x)$, with a simpler distribution.

Let me give you an analogy, once explained by Professor Christian Robert from the University of Paris-Dauphine, France, and the University of Warwick, UK.

Imagine you are a visitor in a museum and suddenly there is a blackout. The gallery is completely dark. Your only way to look at the paintings is to use a small torch. The beam of the torch is very narrow so at any time you will only see a small part of the painting. But you can move your torch along the painting until you discover all of it. Then you will have the big picture. Of course, you can argue that a painting is more than the sum of its parts, but that's another story.

The Metropolis-Hastings algorithm

This algorithm will build a sequence of sampled values x_l, such that this sequence will converge to $p(x)$. So the chain of values is a sample of $p(x)$ and these values are approximately distributed according to $p(x)$. However, at the beginning, and because each value is dependent on its previous value, the first samples are also very dependent on the initial value x_0. It is therefore recommended not to use the initial values and to give a period of warm-up to the algorithm.

We recall a similar result in the previous algorithm. Based on the Markov Chain, it is possible to show that, even if it's hard to determine when the algorithm will reach stationarity, the average of the sampled values will converge almost surely to $E(f)$, the empirical average defined by:

$$\tilde{E}(f) = \frac{1}{L} \sum_{l=1}^{L} f\left(x^{(l)}\right)$$

This will converge almost surely to $E(f)$. We recall that almost sure convergence is defined as a sequence $X_1, X_2, ..., X_n$ of random variables converging to a random variable X if:

$$p\left(\left\{s \in S : \lim_{n \to \infty} X_n(s) = X(s)\right\}\right) = 1$$

Of course, we can't feasibly sample an infinite sequence of variables, but we have a guarantee it will converge. So in theory we know it will converge and therefore sampling from the Markov chain is equivalent to *iid* sampling from the distribution. In practice, we need to sample a lot to get good results.

The Metropolis-Hastings algorithm works as follows:

1. Draw a value $x_t \sim q(x_t \mid x_{t-1})$ where $q(x)$ is our simple proposal distribution.
2. Compute the probability of acceptance with:

$$\rho\left(x_t, x_{t-1}\right) = \min\left\{1, \frac{\tilde{p}\left(x_t\right)}{\tilde{p}\left(x_{t-1}\right)} \frac{q\left(x_{t-1} \mid x_t\right)}{q\left(x_t \mid x_{t-1}\right)}\right\}$$

3. Take x_t with probability $\rho(x_t, x_{t-1})$ and x_{t-1} with probability $1 - \rho(x_t, x_{t-1})$.

Given the choice of $q(x)$, this algorithm will preserve the stationarity of the distribution $p(x)$ in the Markov chain. In theory, again, this algorithm is guaranteed to converge for an arbitrary distribution $q(x)$. This is an impressive result, hence the popularity of this algorithm. However, in practice, things are a bit more complicated because the convergence might happen very late in the process, if for example the proposal distribution $q(x)$ is too narrow. On the other hand, a too large distribution might end up with a very unstable algorithm. It will still converge but with a huge step and can miss the most important part of the original distribution $p(x)$ by leaving the area with high probability mass too early.

The sequence of samples x_t represents a random walk and we can illustrate the previous problem of practical convergence by looking at what happens to such a trajectory in a simple example.

We want to sample from a two-dimensional Gaussian distribution and we use a smaller two-dimensional Gaussian as the proposal distribution. In order to deal with multi-dimensional Gaussian, we need the MASS package:

```
library(MASS)
bigauss <- mvrnorm(50000, mu = c(0, 0), Sigma = matrix(c(1, .1, .1, 1),
2))

bigauss.estimate <- kde2d(bigauss[,1], bigauss[,2], n = 50)

contour(bigauss.estimate,nlevels=6,lty=2)
```

This code snippet plots a simple two-dimensional Gaussian distribution as shown next. From there, we will use a smaller Gaussian distribution whose next mean value will be drawn from the current small Gaussian distribution. This is not yet an application of the Metropolis-Hastings algorithm, but just an example to visualize what happens with different covariance to the random walk and where it can go in just a few iterations.

The starting point of the random walk is arbitrarily in the center of the big Gaussian distribution, that is, at coordinates (0,0) in this case:

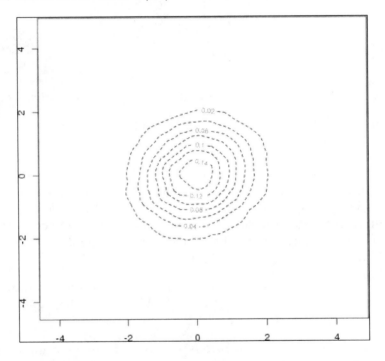

The following figure shows the small proposal distribution in red contour lines:

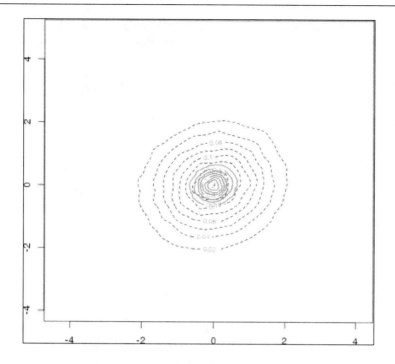

The following code draws random samples from the small distribution in the center and updates its center with the previous value:

```
L <- 10
smallcov <- matrix(c(.1,.01,.01,.1),2)
x <- c(0,0)
for(i in 1:L)
{
  x2 <- mvrnorm(1, mu=x, Sigma=smallcov)
  lines(c(x[1],x2[1]), c(x[2],x2[2]), t='p',pch=20)
  x <- x2
}
```

We show three examples, with 10, 100, and 1,000 points. Obviously, a pure random walk is completely off the initial big distribution after a few iterations. As for 1,000 iterations, they are totally off:

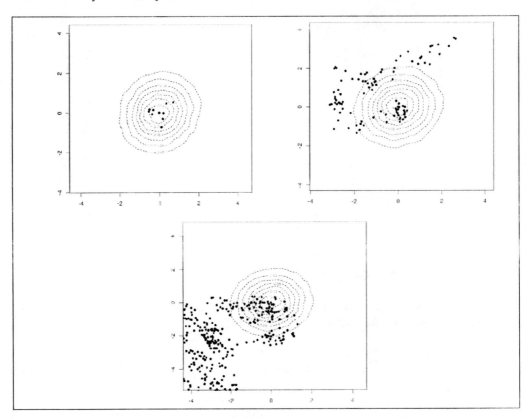

Now, let's complete the picture and implement the last bit of the Metropolis-Hastings algorithm in R. As we assumed that we can estimate *p(x)* on our target distribution, we will use here the dmvnorm function from the mvtnorm package.

To illustrate the behavior of this algorithm, we will take a simple Gaussian distribution as *p(x)* and an even simpler uniform distribution as *q(x)*.

So the proposal distribution is simply:

$$q\left(x_t \mid x_{t-1}\right) = \frac{1}{2\alpha} I\left(x_{t-1} - \alpha, x_{t-1} + \alpha\right)(x)$$

And $p(x) = N(0,1)$, a simple Gaussian distribution:

```
p = function(x)
{
  dnorm(x,0,1)
}


mh = function(x,alpha)
{
  xt <- runif(1,x-alpha,x+alpha)
  if( runif(1) > p(xt) / p(x) )
    xt <- x

  return(xt)
}


sampler = function(L,alpha)
{
  x <- numeric(L)
  for(i in 2:L)
    x[i] <- mh(x[i-1],alpha)

  return(x)
}


par(mfrow=c(2,2))
for(l in c(10,100,1000,10000))
{
  hist(sampler(l,1),main=paste(l,"iterations"),breaks=50,freq=F,xlim=c(-
4,4),ylim=c(0,1))
  lines(x0,p(x0))
}
```

The first function is the evaluation of $p(x)$. Then it is followed by the Metropolis-Hastings step using the proposal uniform distribution defined before.

Then we implement the sampler, which takes two parameters: L is the number of iterations and `alpha` the width of the uniform distribution. The bigger alpha is, the larger the area this proposal distribution will cover. Too large a value will result in too many jumps and poor results. Too small a value will have a serious impact on the numerical convergence of the algorithm, even if we know that theoretically it will converge.

Then the last part of the code draws some results for 10, 100, 1,000, and 10,000 iterations. Running this code, we obtain the following graph. Your results will be different because we draw numbers at random, of course, but the overall plot is similar:

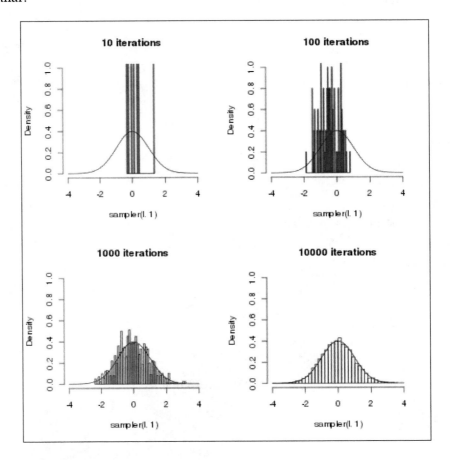

It is clear that, with only 10 iterations, the results are poor. After a warm-up period of 100 iterations, it seems we are close to the mean value, but the variance of such a dataset will be completely off with respect to $p(x)$. After 1,000 iterations, our dataset begins to be quite close to the target distribution. Finally, after 10,000 iterations, we have a superb histogram.

Next, we vary `alpha`, with 1,000 iterations. We use the following code:

```
par(mfrow=c(2,2))

for(a in c(0.1,0.5,1,10))

{

        hist(sampler(1000,a),main=paste("alpha=",a),breaks=50,freq=F,xlim
=c(-4,4),ylim=c(0,1))

        lines(x0,p(x0))

}
```

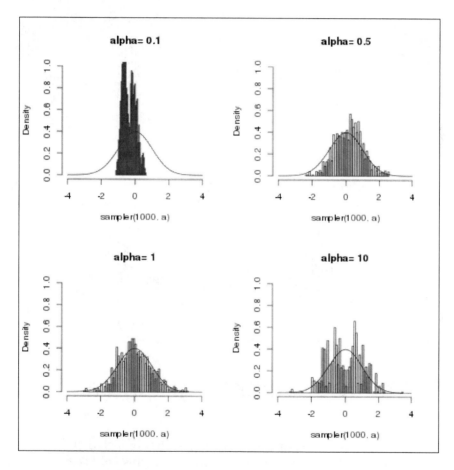

Again, we see interesting results: the theory says it will converge. The practice needs a bit of tuning first. It seems that *alpha=0.5* or *alpha=1* are large enough to cover the distribution. However, *alpha=0.1* is too narrow and can't explore the space fast enough in only 1,000 iterations. On the other hand, *alpha=10* gives a bi-modal distribution; the jumps are too big.

If we run the same experiment with many more iterations, such as 50,000, we see a stabilization of the algorithm and most of the proposal distribution seem to converge to the ideal solution. Again, *alpha=0.1* and *alpha=10* seem a bit weak, but the overall result is more than acceptable this time:

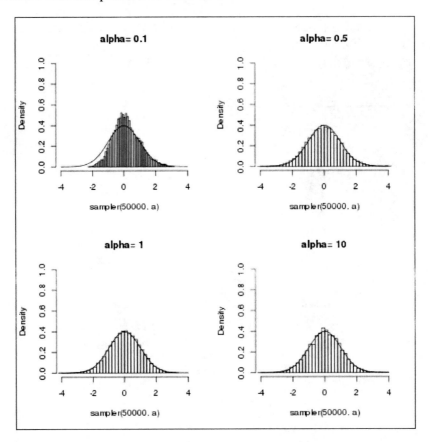

MCMC for probabilistic graphical models in R

In fact, this section could be the title of book. As a matter of fact, there are several books entirely devoted to this specific topic. Research in this field is extremely active, with many new algorithms coming every year.

There are numerous packages implementing MCMC algorithms for different types of algorithms. There are also more generic frameworks such as the famous BUGS (and its open source implementation OpenBUGS) and a new, even more powerful framework called Stan. Historically, BUGS was the first framework to popularize MCMC inference in Bayesian statistics and literally led to a revolution in this field, as everyone could benefit from Bayesian statistics right out of the box.

Making an introduction to each of them and showing all the possibilities of MCMC for a few specific graphical models would require another book as big as this one. In this section, we will therefore focus on a programming environment available in R. In fact, it works also with C++, Python, Matlab, Julia, Stata, and even on the command line! It allows the implementation of all sorts of Bayesian models, as we have seen so far. Stan mainly uses MCMC algorithms to perform inferences.

Installing Stan and RStan

This procedure is detailed on the following web page: `https://github.com/stan-dev/rstan/wiki/Rstan-Getting-Started`.

Thus we will just recall the basic steps in order to install Stan and RStan:

```
Sys.setenv(MAKEFLAGS = "-j4")

install.packages("rstan", dependencies = TRUE)
```

Prepare yourself for a long installation, as Stan will need numerous packages. Finally, depending on your R installation, you might have to restart R, but in general it is not necessary.

Finally, load RStan like any other package:

```
library(rstan)
```

You should see an introductory message such as this, telling you Stan is ready:

```
Loading required package: ggplot2

rstan (Version 2.9.0, packaged: 2016-01-05 16:17:47 UTC, GitRev:
05c3d0058b6a)

For execution on a local, multicore CPU with excess RAM we recommend
calling

rstan_options(auto_write = TRUE)

options(mc.cores = parallel::detectCores())
```

A simple example in RStan

We show here some basic possibilities in RStan. The reader is encouraged to read more about it and try more examples.

RStan is based on a probabilistic programming language used to describe the Bayesian models. For example, we can make a simple univariate Gaussian model:

```
parameters
{
        real y;
}


model
{
        y ~ normal(0,1);
}
```

This code is Stan code, not R code. Then, in R, we can simulate this model, by doing:

```
fit = stan(file='example.stan')
```

The model will be simulated using an MCMC algorithm and the results are displayed using:

```
print(fit)
Inference for Stan model: example.
4 chains, each with iter=2000; warmup=1000; thin=1;
post-warmup draws per chain=1000, total post-warmup draws=4000.


      mean se_mean   sd  2.5%   25%   50%   75% 97.5% n_eff Rhat
y     0.00    0.03 0.98 -1.93 -0.63 -0.01  0.64  1.98  1191    1
lp__ -0.48    0.02 0.69 -2.35 -0.63 -0.20 -0.05  0.00  1718    1


Samples were drawn using NUTS(diag_e)
For each parameter, n_eff is a crude measure of effective sample size,
and Rhat is the potential scale reduction factor on split chains (at
convergence, Rhat=1).
```

It's interesting to see that this package has indeed a warm-up procedure as we saw before and it tries to compute an estimate of the effective sample size for a simple Gaussian. The value of 1191 (the n_eff column) is not too far from the examples we saw in the previous section.

Summary

In this chapter, we saw the second (and presumably most successful) approach to performing Bayesian inference, with algorithms such as rejection and importance sampling, which are based on the use of a proposal distribution simpler than the one we want to estimate.

These two algorithms are usually efficient with low-dimensional cases but suffer from long convergence problems, when they converge at all, in high dimensions.

We then introduced the most important algorithm in Bayesian inference: the MCMC method using the Metropolis-Hastings algorithm. This algorithm is extremely versatile and has a nice property: it converges toward the distribution one wants to simulate. However, it needs careful tuning in order to converge, but its convergence is guaranteed in theory.

In the next chapter, we will explore the most standard statistical model ever: linear regression. While it seems beyond the scope of this book, this model is so important that it needs to be introduced. However, we will not stop at the simple form of it but will explore its Bayesian interpretation, how it can be represented as a probabilistic graphical model, and what benefit we get from doing so.

6
Bayesian Modeling – Linear Models

A linear regression model aims at explaining the behavior of one variable with another one, or several others, and by so doing, the assumption is that the relationship between the variables is linear. In general, the expectation of the target variable, the one you need to explain, is an affine transform of several other variables.

Linear models are presumably the most used statistical models, mainly because of their simplicity and the fact they have been studied for decades, leading to all possible extensions and analysis one can imagine. Basically all statistical packages, languages, or software implement linear regression models.

The idea of the model is really simple: a variable y is to be explained by several other variables x_i by assuming a linear combination of x's — that is, a weighted sum of x's.

This model appeared in the 18th century in the work of Roger Joseph Boscovich. Then again, his method has been used by Pierre-Simon de Laplace, Adrien-Marie Legendre, and Carl Friedrich Gauss. It seems that Francis Galton, a mathematical genius of the 19th century, coined the term "linear regression".

The model is generally written as a linear combination of variables as follows:

$$y = \beta_0 + \beta_1 x_1 + \beta_2 x_2 + \ldots + \beta_n x_n + \epsilon.$$

Here, y is the variable to explain, the x's are the explaining variables, and ϵ is a random noise that can be explained by the x's. It is generally a Gaussian-distributed random variable of mean 0 and variance σ_2.

What does it mean in practice? The intuition behind this model is that each x after being rescaled will contribute a little bit to y. In other words, y is made of a sum of little pieces, each being an x.

There are many ways to estimate the value of the parameters from a dataset, and obviously in many situations the value of each parameter is of the utmost importance and needs to be carefully studied. The most used method is the least square method in which one tries to minimize the difference between the real y and its approximation by a sum of x's. Indeed, representing y as a sum of other variables is, as with many models, just an approximation of the reality. Many mathematical tools and algorithms have been developed for linear regression to answer the question of the quality of the model and its parameters.

[The word *difference* is just an analogy. In this case, the correct term is mean squared error, of course.]

In this chapter, we will quickly cover the basics of linear regression. A full-scale study would be beyond the scope of this book and we assume the reader has been exposed to such models before.

The aim of this chapter is to go further and give a Bayesian flavor to the linear regression. In fact, in the standard model, one only focuses on the expectation of y and the parameters. But as soon as each of these components is considered as a random variable, it is possible to explain the linear regression in a Bayesian way and open oneself to many new techniques and benefits of dealing with full-probability distribution instead of just their expectations.

We will review the following elements in this chapter:

- What is a linear regression and how to use it in R?
- What are the main hypotheses in a linear regression and what to do when they break?
- How to compute the parameters by hand and in R
- How to interpret a linear regression as a probabilistic graphical model
- How to estimate the parameters in the Bayesian way and what's the benefit of doing so?
- A review of R packages for Bayesian linear regression
- What is over-fitting, why is it so important to avoid it, and what is the Bayesian solution to it?

Linear regression

We start by looking at the most simple and most used model in statistics, which consists of fitting a straight line to a dataset. We assume we have a data set of pairs (x_i, y_i) that are $i.i.d$ and we want to fit a model such that:

$$y = \beta x + \beta_0 + \epsilon$$

Here, ϵ is a Gaussian noise. If we assume that $x_i \in \mathbb{R}^n$ then the expected value can also be written as:

$$\hat{y} = \beta_0 + \sum_{i=1}^{n} x_i \beta_i$$

Or, in matrix notation, we can also include the intercept β_0 into the vector of parameters and add a column on 1 in X, such that $X = (1, x_1, ..., x_n)$ to finally obtain:

$$\hat{y} = X^T \beta$$

The following figure shows an example (in one dimension) of a data set with its corresponding regression line:

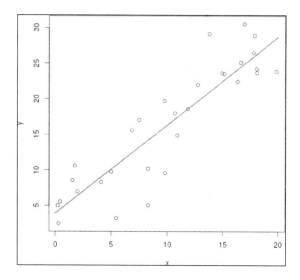

In R, fitting a linear model is an easy task, as we will see now. Here, we produce a small data set with an artificial number, in order to reproduce the previous figure. In R, the function to fit a linear model is `lm()` and it is the workhorse of this language in many situations. Of course, later in this chapter we will see more advanced algorithms:

```
N=30
x=runif(N,0,20)
```

```
y= 1.2*x + 4 + rnorm(N,0,4)
plot(x,y)
m=lm(y~x)
xx=seq(0,20,1)
lines(xx,xx*m$coefficients[2]+m$coefficients[1],col=2,lw=2)
```

In this example, we generate 30 random points between 0 and 20. Then we compute y, on a straight line of slope 1.2 and intercept 4, adding a random noise, with zero mean at a variance of 4.

We compute the model in m with the function `lm()`. Finally we plot the result.

Printing the variable m gives the following result:

```
Call:
lm(formula = y ~ x)


Coefficients:
(Intercept)                x
      3.919            1.238
```

Here we see that the intercept is 3.919, close to the value of 4, and the slope is 1.238, also close to 1.2. As we added an important noise (of variance 4), it is not surprising to see a difference between the theoretical model and the fitted model.

Estimating the parameters

In order to estimate the parameters, we need a discrepancy measure, or in other words, a function that measures some sort of difference between the model and the data set. Of course, the goal is to minimize this difference. Here the word *difference* has a very broad meaning and many functions could work. However, it has been found that one of the most useful and practical is the mean squared error defined by:

$$MSE = \left\| Y - X^T \tilde{\beta} \right\|_2^2 = \frac{1}{N} \sum_{i=1}^{N} \left(y_i - \sum_{j=1}^{n} x_j \beta_j \right)^2$$

To estimate the parameters of the model, we resort to a method we saw earlier, called the maximum likelihood. The likelihood is the probability of observing a data set given some parameters, in this case. We assume as usual the data are identically and independently distributed. This allows us to write the maximum likelihood as follows:

$$\hat{\theta} = argmax_\theta \, p(D \mid \theta)$$

Here, θ is the set of all parameters $\theta = \{\beta_1, \ldots \beta_p\}$.

Basically we want to find the parameters that maximize this probability. As we assume *i.i.d* data, we can write:

$$\hat{\theta} = argmax_\theta \prod_{i=1}^{N} p(y_i \mid x_i \theta)$$

Then, to simplify the computations we take the log-likelihood and have a sum instead of a big product:

$$\hat{\theta} = argmax_\theta \sum_{i=1}^{N} p(y_i \mid x_i \theta)$$

Next, we need an analytical form for the probability and in the linear regression, we saw the target data is Gaussian distributed as follows:

$$p(y \mid x\theta) = N(y \mid X^T \theta, \sigma^2)$$

If in the log-likelihood we replace the probability with the density function of a Gaussian, we will obtain:

$$\log L(\theta) = \sum_{i=1}^{N} \log \left[\left(\frac{1}{2\pi\sigma^2} \right)^{\frac{1}{2}} \exp \left(\frac{-\left(y_i - \beta^T X_i\right)^2}{2\sigma^2} \right) \right]$$

$$= \sum_{i=1}^{N} \left[\log \left(\frac{1}{2\pi\sigma^2} \right)^{\frac{1}{2}} + \log \exp \left(\frac{-\left(y_i - \beta^T X_i\right)^2}{2\sigma^2} \right) \right]$$

$$= \sum_{i=1}^{N} \log \left(\frac{1}{2\pi\sigma^2} \right)^{\frac{1}{2}} - \sum_{i=1}^{N} \frac{\left(y_i - \beta^T X_i\right)^2}{2\sigma^2}$$

$$= \frac{N}{2} \log \frac{1}{2\pi\sigma^2} - \frac{1}{2\sigma^2} \sum_{i=1}^{N} \left(y_i - \beta^T X_i\right)^2$$

This long development leads to two terms in the last equation; one is the constant and the other one depends on the parameters. As our goal is to maximize this expression, we can get rid of the constant term without loss of generality. And because it easier (in most numerical packages) to minimize a function than to maximize it, we will take the negative of this:

$$NLL(\theta) = \frac{1}{2} \sum_{i=1}^{N} \left(y_i - \beta^T X_i \right)^2$$

And we find the famous results again: the maximum likelihood estimator for a linear regression model is nothing but minimizing the square error!

In order to find the solution, we need to do a bit more linear algebra again. First we write this expression in matrix form to make things simpler:

$$NLL(\theta) = \frac{1}{2} (y - X\beta)^T (y - X\beta)$$

Here, X is the design matrix — that is, the matrix of all the data set. Each row i of the matrix is a vector $\left(x_1^{(i)}, \dots, x_p^{(i)} \right)$. This form is very convenient so that we deal with the sum from within the scalar product.

After expanding this expression we obtain:

$$NLL(\theta) = \frac{1}{2} \beta^T X^T X \beta + \frac{1}{2} \left(y^T y - y^T X \beta - \beta^T X^T y \right)$$

This again can be simplified. Indeed, we are only interested in the term dependent on the parameters. So the rest can be discarded. Moreover, we know that $y \in \mathbb{R}^N$ and the same for $\beta^T X^T$ so we can write $y^T X \beta = \beta^T X^T y$, which helps us to simplify the main expression again to finally obtain:

$$NLL(\theta) = \frac{1}{2} \beta^T X^T X \beta - \beta^T X^T y$$

The minimum of this convex function is reached when its first derivative (in fact the Jacobian matrix) is equal to 0. So we derive it and obtain:

$$\frac{\partial NLL(\theta)}{\partial \beta} = \left(X^T X\right)\beta - X^T y$$

Solving this equation to zero, the solution is finally:

$$\hat{\beta} = \left(X^T X\right)^{-1} X^T y$$

This is what the function `lm()` computes in R and most numerical languages or packages. However, we advise you not to implement it directly, especially when the data set is big. Indeed, inverting such a matrix like that could lead to a numerical instability that is hard to control.

The main problem when doing linear regression arises when the parameters are not stable and a little change can have massive effects on parameters. This could be due to collinearity between parameters, parameters canceling each other, or many other reasons.

One technique to solve this problem is known as shrinkage and its goal is to constrain the parameters to that they don't grow too far away. This usually gives better models with better predictive power. One simple approach to shrinkage is to put a Gaussian prior on the parameters. This technique is called **ridge regression** or **L2 penalization**.

Practically speaking, we assume the following priors on the parameters:

$$p(\beta) = \prod_j N\left(\beta_j \mid 0, \tau^2\right)$$

Here, τ controls the amount of shrinkage one wants to apply to the model and the Gaussian distributions are zero-centered. The last point means we want the parameters not to go too far away from 0.

So, the optimization problem to solve becomes the following:

$$argmax_\beta \sum_{i=1}^{N} \log N\left(y_i \mid \beta_0 + \beta^T x_i, \sigma^2\right) + \sum_{j=1}^{D} \log N\left(\beta_j \mid 0, \tau^2\right)$$

To be brief, we give the solution directly, because the calculus is similar to the previous development. The negative log-likelihood is therefore:

$$NLL(\theta) = \frac{1}{N}(y - X^T \beta)^T (y - X^T \beta) + \lambda \|\beta\|_2^2$$

The only difference, really, is that the last term: $\lambda = \dfrac{\sigma^2}{\tau^2}$ controls the amount of penalization. The higher this term, the more the parameters will be penalized when they grow too much. A good amount of penalization can lead some of the parameters to become close to zero. In that case, it can be a good idea to try to fit the model again without those parameters. In a sense, it is a method for variable selection. A large τ will reduce λ, which follows the intuition that, if the prior on the parameters has a large variance, then, a broad range of values can be reached. If the variance is, on the contrary small then only a smaller range will have a high probability to be reached.

The solution to this optimization problem is:

$$\beta_{ridge} = (\lambda I_D + X^T X)^{-1} X^T y$$

Again, we advise you not to compute this directly in R but rather to rely on packages that have been specifically implemented to be numerically stable. We recommend two packages:

- MASS with the function `lm.ridge()`, which is similar to `lm()`
- `glmnet` with its function, `glmnet()`

The second package implements several algorithms. You can use it for ridge regression, and for L1-penalization (Lasso). In L1-penalization, instead of using a Gaussian prior on the parameters, we have a Laplace prior. The Laplace distribution is very peaky in the center and this has a particular effect: collinear parameters can reach the value 0 exactly. In that case, they are simply eliminated from the model. It's a very powerful variable selection method.

However, the problem doesn't have an analytical solution and needs a specific optimization algorithm to find the solution.

In R, we can fit a model with `lm()` and `glmnet()` as follows, where we use the `mtcars` data set included in R directly, where we want to regress the variable `mpg` against the other variables:

```
m1 <- lm( mpg ~ . , mtcars)
m1
Call:
lm(formula = mpg ~ ., data = mtcars)

Coefficients:
(Intercept)          cyl            disp              hp            drat
wt
   12.30337      -0.11144         0.01334        -0.02148         0.78711
-3.71530
       qsec            vs              am            gear            carb
    0.82104       0.31776         2.52023         0.65541        -0.19942
```

We can plot the model and see the theoretical line with the real data set:

```
yhat <- ( as.matrix(mtcars[2:10] ) %*% m1$coefficients[2:10] ) +
m1$coefficients[1]
```

Also note that we use the scalar product `%*%`:

```
plot(sort(mtcars$mpg)); lines(sort(yhat),col=2)
```

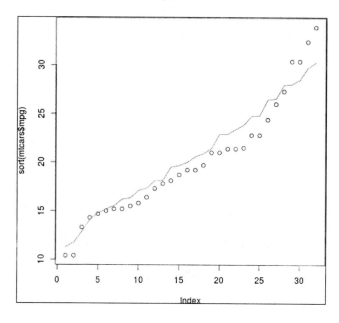

Bayesian linear models

In this section, we are going to extend the standard linear regression model using the Bayesian paradigm. One of the goals is to put prior knowledge on the parameters of the models to help to solve the over-fitting problem.

Over-fitting a model

One immense benefit of going Bayesian when doing a linear model is to have better control of the parameters. Let's do an initial experiment to see what happens when the parameters are completely out of control.

We are going to generate a simple model in R and look at the parameters when they are fitted with the standard approach for linear models.

Let's first generate some data points at random to obtain 10 variables and plot them:

```
N <- 30
x <- runif(N, -2, 2)
X <- cbind(rep(1, N), x, x^2, x^3, x^4, x^5, x^6, x^7, x^8)
matplot(X, t='l')
```

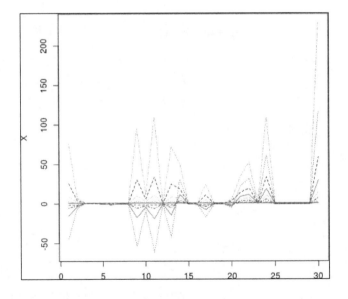

Next we generate the dependent variable following the model:

$$y = X\beta + \epsilon$$

Here, ϵ is a Gaussian noise of variance σ_2. We use the following code in R and plot the variable y. As we use randomly generated numbers, your plot might be different from the one in this book:

```
sigma <- 10
eps <- rnorm(N, mean = 0, sd = sigma)
y <- X %*% true_beta + eps
plot(y, t='l')
```

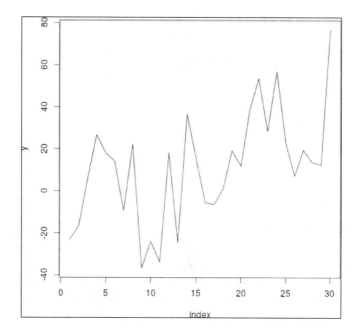

Then we estimate the coefficients of the model with the `lm()` function:

```
model <- lm(y~., data=data.frame(X[,2:ncol(X)]))
beta_hat <- model$coefficients
```

We plot the true coefficients and the estimated coefficients to see, visually, how close they are. And the result is … not good!

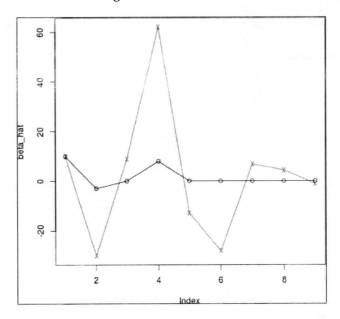

If we have a closer look at the values, we can clearly see that the model tried to use all the variables when we gave them a zero coefficient in the true model. Moreover, it tried to compensate between all the variables, hence the positive and negative values all along the vector of parameters. Your results might be different from the values shown here, because we use random data, but the behavior will be similar:

```
> true_beta
[1] 10 -3  0  8  0  0  0  0  0
> beta_hat
(Intercept)           x         V2           V3          V4          V5
V6          V7          V8
  10.012121  -30.091272    8.904295    62.005179  -12.913125  -28.102293

   6.844616    4.410177   -1.154756
```

In fact, most of the values are terribly wrong. This is a perfect example of over-fitting. The model tried to fit the data perfectly, ending in something completely off:

```
> true_beta
[1] 10 -3 0 8 0 0 0 0 0
> beta_hat
```

```
(Intercept) x V2 V3 V4 V5 V6 V7 V8
10.012121 -30.091272 8.904295 62.005179 -12.913125 -28.102293
6.844616 4.410177 -1.154756
```

In this case, we knew the true values beforehand but, in practice, we try to fit a model on a dataset to find out good values for the parameters. As we saw in the previous section, one good technique is called regularization and it is equivalent to placing prior distribution on the parameters. By doing so, we somehow constrain the parameters to stay within an acceptable range of values, with a higher probability.

Graphical model of a linear model

Before going further, we need to visualize the structure of a linear mode and better understand the relationships between variables. We can, of course, represent it as a probabilistic graphical model.

The linear model captures the relationships between observable variables x and a target variable y. This relation is modeled by a set of parameters θ. But remember the distribution of y for each data point indexed by i:

$$yi \sim N(X_i\beta, \sigma^2)$$

Here, X_i is a row vector for which the first element is always 1 to capture the intercept of the linear model. If you look at earlier pages in this chapter, you will realize that the linear model has been written with many different forms that are all equivalent. We leave it to the reader as an exercise to show they are all equivalent. For example, X_i could be a column vector, and so on.

So our first graphical model could be as follows:

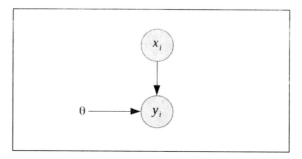

The parameter θ is itself composed of the intercept, the coefficients β for each component of X, and the variance σ^2 in the distribution of y_i:

So, this decomposition leads us to a second version of the graphical model in which we explicitly separate the components of θ:

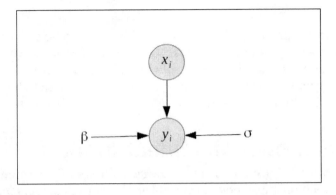

We introduce again *plate notation* in probabilistic graphical models. When a rectangle is drawn around a set of nodes with a number or a variable in a corner (*N* for example), it means the same graph is repeated many times.

The likelihood function of a linear model is:

$$L(\theta) = \prod_{i=1}^{N} p(y_i \mid X_i, \beta, \sigma)$$

This form is representable as a graphical model and, based on the previous graph, we finally have:

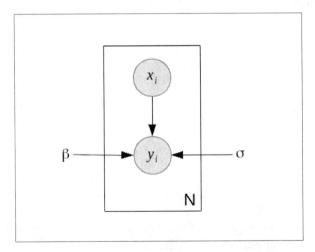

In this graph, it is clearly stated that each y_i is dependent on one x_i. It is also clear that the parameters $\theta = \{\beta, \sigma\}$ are all shared as they are outside the plate.

For the sake of simplicity, we will keep β as a vector, but you could also decompose it into its univariate components and use the plate notation for those:

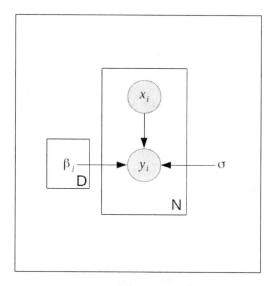

In the last two iterations of the graphical model, we see that the parameter β could have a prior probability on it instead of being fixed. In fact, the parameter σ can also be considered as a random variable. For the time being, we will keep it fixed.

Posterior distribution

Many prior distributions could be used for β but they need to be tractable or simply have an appropriate meaning in the context of a linear regression. Here we need a distribution that has a zero mean, is symmetric, and has an infinite support. The reasons are:

- Zero-mean because we want our parameters to be driven toward zero if possible; this is the shrinkage effect. So we give the highest mass of probability to the center at zero.

- Symmetric because we want to give equal chances for positive and negative values. A priori, we don't know which direction the parameters will take.

- Infinite support because we don't want to block the parameters to have certain values. Obviously, with most of the probability mass in the center, the tail of the distribution, despite having an infinite support, will have a low probability. So we are trying to force the model not to have huge values like we saw in the previous example.

- The distribution needs to be simple enough that we can compute the posterior of the parameters and the predictive posterior of y.

Given all these reasons, the Gaussian distribution seems to be a good candidate for our purpose.

The conditional distribution for y is as usual:

$$p\left(y_i \mid X_i \beta \sigma^2\right) = N\left(y_i \mid X\beta, \sigma^2\right)$$

We remember we saw that the **Maximum Likelihood Estimator (MLE)** is:

$$\hat{\beta} = \left(X^T X\right)^{-1} X^T y$$

And the estimator for the variance can also be estimated (left as an exercise) and is:

$$\hat{\sigma} = \frac{1}{N} \sum_{i=1}^{N} \left(y_i - \hat{\beta}^T X_i\right)^2$$

The good thing about having a Gaussian prior on the parameters is that it is conjugate to the likelihood function. It means that the posterior of the parameters is also a Gaussian distribution such that:

$$p\left(\beta \mid yX\sigma\tau\right) \propto p\left(y \mid \beta X \sigma\tau\right) p\left(\beta \mid \tau\right) = N\left(\beta \mid m, S\right)$$

Here:

$$m = \sigma^{-2} S X^T y$$

$$S = \left(\tau I + \sigma^{-2} X^T X\right)^{-1}$$

Here we find again the τ parameter, which controls how large the prior is on the parameters. It is the same parameter τ we used in the previous section on ridge regression. In fact, it can be shown that having Gaussian priors on the parameter β and the ridge regression are equivalent. The reader is encouraged to take the previous two formulas and calculate again the ridge regression to see the relation between the two.

Finally, the last thing we need to do is to compute the posterior predictive distribution. The posterior predictive distribution is the distribution of an unknown y when some Xs have been observed after computing the parameters. It is basically making a prediction with a model that has been learned with the previous method.

The reason it is important is because we do a complete Bayesian treatment of the problem, instead of a pure statistical one. In the standard linear model, the scalar product of X and β is sufficient to compute the expected value of y when we wish to make a prediction.

In other words, after finding the β parameters we simply do:

$$y_j = \sum_{i=1}^{N} x_i . \beta_i$$

But because here we have a full Bayesian model, instead of just having the expectation of y, we have the full probability distribution. As we will see, the posterior distribution is also a Gaussian, and a Gaussian is defined by its mean and variance. Therefore, by using a full Bayesian model, we also compute the posterior variance and have an estimation of the uncertainty of the prediction:

$$p\left(y' \mid y\tau\sigma^2 X\right) = \int p\left(y' \mid \beta\sigma^2\right) p\left(\beta \mid y\tau\sigma^2\right) d\beta$$
$$= N\left(y' \mid m^T X', \sigma^2\left(X'\right)\right)$$

Here:

$$\sigma^2\left(X'\right) = \sigma^2 + X'^T S X'$$

X' and y' are respectively the new observed data upon which we want to do the prediction y'.

Finally, we can draw the graphical model for the full Bayesian interpretation of the linear model:

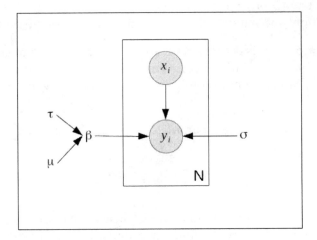

In fact, we only presented the case when the prior on β is Gaussian, but other priors such as a Laplace distribution can be used. This leads to an L1-penalization that doesn't have an analytical form. However, a very efficient algorithm called the **Lasso** can be used to find the parameters. A very efficient implementation of it can be found in the `glmnet` package.

Implementation in R

Let's take an example from the beginning of this chapter again. When we tried to compute the parameters, we found strange values that were seriously off from their true value, meaning there was a problem in the estimation procedure. We saw that this problem is called over-fitting.

Then we looked at a solution by interpreting the linear model in the Bayesian framework and calculated the solutions of the problem.

Implementing it is really easy when the priors on the parameters are Gaussian:

```
dimension <- length(true_beta)
lambda <- diag(0.1, dimension, dimension)
posterior_sigma <- sigma^2 * solve(t(X) %*% X + sigma^2 * lambda)
posterior_beta  <- sigma^(-2) * as.vector(posterior_sigma %*% (t(X) %*%
y))
```

The posterior parameters are now:

```
 posterior_beta
[1]   7.76069781 -0.06509725   1.18834799   2.72321814   0.16637478
2.65759764
[7]  -0.10993147 -0.31961733   0.02273269
```

This is far better than what we had before. But it is still not perfect. Indeed, the true β parameters are:

```
true_beta <- c(10, -3, 0, 8, 0, 0, 0, 0, 0)
```

And we can see that the second parameter is too small and many parameters are too high, with values going from 1 to 2 when they should be zero.

Indeed, the penalization in the form of the `lambda` variable is too weak. It means the variance is too large. We can therefore give more penalization by doing:

```
lambda <- 0.5 * diag(0.1, dimension, dimension)
```

We then recompute the results:

```
 posterior_beta
[1]   9.6677088 -0.7393309   1.1248994   3.5526708 -0.1869873   2.8805658
-0.3506464
[8]  -0.4582813   0.1190531
```

It is not perfect but the intercept is now closer to 10 (9.66) and the second parameter now has a better value. The other parameters are still off but they are going in the right direction.

We can penalize even more and run the same code again:

```
lambda <- 0.1*diag(0.1, dimension, dimension)
posterior_sigma <- sigma^2 * solve(t(X) %*% X + sigma^2 * lambda)
posterior_beta   <- sigma^(-2) * as.vector(posterior_sigma %*% (t(X) %*%
y))
posterior_beta
[1] 12.0750175 -3.8736938   0.6105363   8.0942494 -1.0959572   1.3938047
-0.1099443
[8]  -0.3496412   0.1280143
```

Despite it not being perfect, we see that we are closer to the true solution. Needless to say, the example we used has been specifically made to be hard to solve. Despite this, the Bayesian solution is able to converge to the true solution, where the simple linear regression was completely wrong.

After running the previous model, we can plot the results with the following code:

```
t <- seq(-2,2,0.01)
T <- cbind(rep(1, N), t, t^2, t^3, t^4, t^5, t^6, t^7, t^8)


plot(x,y, xlim=c(-2,2), ylim=range(y, T%*%true_beta))
lines(t,T%*%true_beta, col='black', lwd=3)
lines(t,T%*%beta_hat,  col='blue',  lwd=3)
lines(t,T%*%posterior_beta, col='red', lwd=3)


legend('topleft', c('True function', 'OLS estimate', 'Bayesian
estimate'), col=c('black','blue','red'), lwd=3)
```

The first two lines generate evenly spaced data points to draw the results. Then the first plot draws the dataset (little black circles). Then we draw three curves on it:

- **In black**: This is the true model as defined in the R program
- **In blue**: This is the OLS estimate (the standard linear regression)
- **In red**: This is the Bayesian estimate with the penalization we found earlier

The blue curve (OLS estimate) tries to follow the data points as much as possible, fitting more noise and being far away from the true function. This is a good example of over-fitting.

On the contrary, the red curve (Bayesian estimate) did a good job finding the true function that generated the data in the beginning:

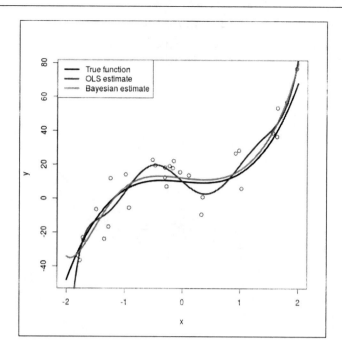

Now we want to add to this graph the 95% posterior predictive interval. Thanks to the Bayesian approach, we can easily compute it from the posterior distribution. Therefore the code in R will be as follows:

```
pred_sigma <- sqrt(sigma^2 + apply((T%*%posterior_sigma)*T, MARGIN=1,
FUN=sum))

upper_bound <- T%*%posterior_beta + qnorm(0.95)*pred_sigma

lower_bound <- T%*%posterior_beta - qnorm(0.95)*pred_sigma
```

The previous code computes the upper and lower bound along the dataset we used. And finally the following code draws the plot:

```
plot(c(0,0),xlim=c(-2,2), ylim=range(y,lower_bound,upper_
bound),col='white')

polygon( c(t,rev(t)), c(upper_bound,rev(lower_bound)), col='grey',
border=NA)

points(x,y)

lines(t,T%*%true_beta, col='black', lwd=3)

lines(t,T%*%beta_hat,  col='blue',  lwd=3)
```

```
lines(t,T%*%posterior_beta, col='red', lwd=3)
legend('topleft', c('True function', 'OLS estimate', 'Bayesian
estimate'), col=c('black','blue','red'), lwd=3)
```

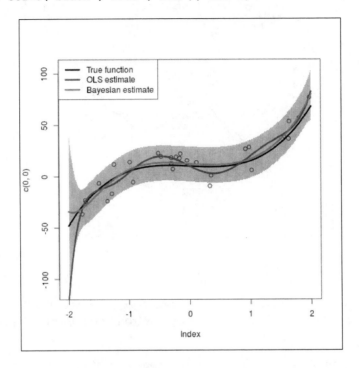

In this code we use the polygon function to draw the gray area representing the 95% predictive interval. We use the qnorm function to compute the values and you can play with theses values to change the interval.

A stable implementation

In the previous implementation, we used the solve() function from R, but it is not always a good idea to inverse a matrix directly as it can quickly lead to numerical instability. As a quick example, here is a little piece of code that generates random invertible matrices and computes the Froebenius distance between an identity matrix and the result of the random matrix multiplied by its inverse. If M is a matrix and M^{-1} its inverse, then $M.M^{-1}=I$. We see in this little example that it is not numerically the case:

```
N <- 200
result <- data.frame(i=numeric(N),fr=numeric(N))


for(i in 2:N)
```

```
{
        x <- matrix(runif(i*i,1,100),i,i)
        y <- t(x)%*%x

        I <- y%*%solve(y)
        I0 <- diag(i)

        fr <- sqrt(sum(diag((I-I0)%*%t(I-I0))))
        result$i[i] <- i
        result$fr[i]<- fr
}
```

The code generates square matrices of size going from 2 x 2 to 200 x 200 and computes the Froebenius distance between a perfect identity matrix and the identity matrix obtained by multiplying the random matrix with its inverse. Plotting the result shows that the distance is not zero all the time:

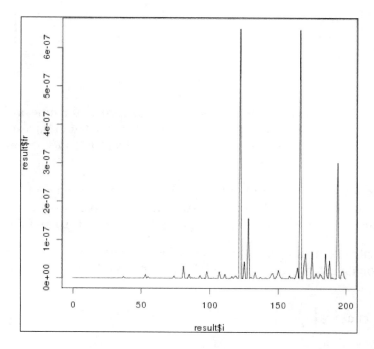

In fact, it increases with the size of the matrix, when more errors accumulate. If we plot the log of the distance, we clearly see the error getting bigger:

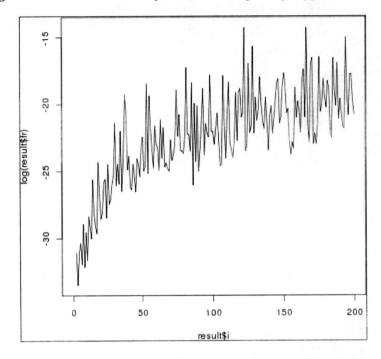

With a perfect inverse matrix, the distance would be zero all the time and therefore the log would be $-$ infinite. So this simple example tells us that in Bayesian linear regression we can have problems when inverting the matrix X. We therefore need a better algorithm.

Here we present a simple algorithm to solve the ridge regression problem with a numerically stable solution. The idea is to transform the problem of matrix inversion into a simpler problem to solve, where the matrix to inverse is triangular.

If X is the matrix containing the data points, and y the vector containing the target, the idea is to first extend the matrix and the vector y as follows:

$$\hat{X} = \begin{pmatrix} X \\ \sqrt{\Lambda} \end{pmatrix} \text{ and } \hat{y} = \begin{pmatrix} y/\sigma \\ 0_D \end{pmatrix} \text{ where } \sqrt{\Lambda} = \frac{1}{\tau}I \text{ and } \Lambda = \frac{1}{\tau^2}I$$

The next step is to do a QR decomposition of $\hat{X}$ and the last step is to compute the inverse of R, which is easier because it's an upper triangular matrix. Finally, the coefficients of the linear regression are given by:

$$\hat{\beta} = R^{-1}Q^T\hat{y}$$

The algorithm in R can be implemented as follows:

```
# the numerically stable function
ridge <- function(X,y,lambda)
{
    tau <- sqrt(lambda)
    Xhat <- rbind(X,(1/tau)*diag(ncol(X)))
    yhat <- c(y,rep(0,ncol(X)))

    aqr <- qr(Xhat)
    q <- qr.Q(aqr)
    r <- qr.R(aqr)

    beta <- solve(r)%*% t(q) %*% yhat

    return(beta)
}
```

This algorithm returns a vector of coefficients, where the first value is the intercept. We assume here that the matrix X has a column of one on the left-hand side. We use the `qr()` function from R to do the QR decomposition.

The following code runs an example:

```
set.seed(300)
N <- 100

# generate some data
x <-runif(N,-2,2)
beta <- c(10,-3,2,-3,0,2,0,0,0)
X <- cbind(rep(1,length(x)), x, x^2, x^3,x^4,x^5,x^6,x^7,x^8)
y <- X %*% beta + rnorm(N,0,4)
```

First of all, we generate random data. The reader will note that for the first time we set the random seed manually so that the following results can be exactly reproduced. The reason for that is that we want to illustrate a nice behavior of the ridge regression.

The code generates random values on the x axis, then we give the true `beta` coefficients, and finally we generate the data.

We also add a random Gaussian noise to the target data y so as to test the capacity of the ridge regression with respect to the standard linear regression solved by an OLS.

The X matrix has many columns but only four of them (plus the intercept) are used to generate y so we expect the linear regression to give very small coefficients to the unused columns (or even zero coefficients).

Then we run the following code to generate results and plot them:

```
# plot the results
t <- seq(-2,2,0.01)
Xt <- cbind(rep(1,length(t)), t, t^2, t^3,t^4,t^5,t^6,t^7,t^8)

yt <- Xt %*% beta
yridge <- Xt %*% ridge(X,y,0.9)

plot(x,y)
lines(t,yt,t='l',lwd=2,lty=2)
lines(t,yridge,col=2,lwd=2)

olsbeta <- lm(y~X-1)
olsy <- Xt %*% olsbeta$coefficients
lines(t, olsy,col=3,lwd=2)
```

First of all, we generate a sequence of points on the x axis, then we compute the X matrix and then the real function called `yt`. This is our theoretical model without noise.

The next step is to compute the ridge regression coefficients with our new `ridge` function as defined previously. Finally, we compute a standard OLS solution to the same problem. And we plot the results:

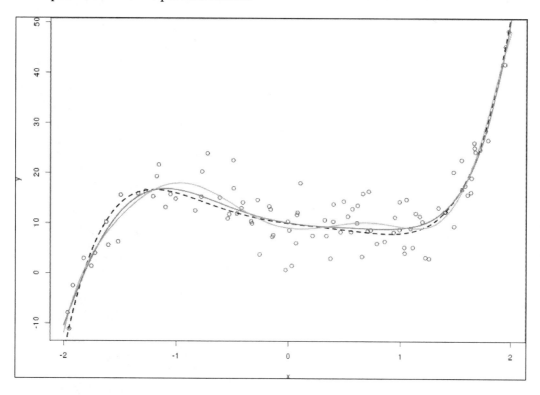

The figure shows the real data set as little circles. The dashed black line is the true function, the one we called our theoretical model before. It is the function without the noise. The red line is very close to the true function. This is the ridge regression. Because of the shrinkage effect of the ridge regression, it is less sensitive to the noise and gives a better solution.

However, the green line is the standard OLS function. It has a wiggly behavior because it is more sensitive to the noise. This is an illustration of the over-fitting problem. In this example, the OLS tries too hard to be close to the data and ends up with a solution that is more unstable than the ridge regression.

In order to illustrate the last point a bit more, we run a final example in which we exaggerate the noise. Instead of having a standard deviation of 4, we use the value 16, making the data very noisy:

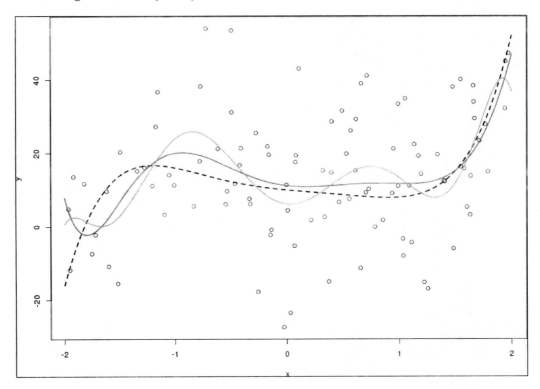

Obviously, this is an extreme example, but we see again that the ridge regression stays closer to the true function. The OLS solution, on the other hand, became completely unstable and is totally over-fitting.

More packages in R

Bayesian linear regression is a well-covered topic in R and many packages implement such models. Of course we mentioned `glmnet` before, which implements ridge regression and Lasso. It also implements a mixture of both, called the elastic net, in which two penalty functions are used at the same time.

Another package is `bayesm`, which covers linear and multivariate linear regression, multinomial logit and probit, mixtures of Gaussians, and even Dirichlet process prior density estimation.

We can also mention the `arm` package, which provides Bayesian versions of `glm()` and `polr()` and implements hierarchical models. It is another very powerful package.

Of course, we shouldn't stop here and ought to extend our study of Bayesian models to all sorts of algorithms and prior distributions. At some point, it becomes impossible to find an analytical solution and one should use Monte-Carlo inference, as we saw in the previous chapter.

Summary

In this chapter, we saw the standard linear model. This model is one of the most important models in statistics and provides a simple, additive way to represent relationships between observed variables and a target.

Estimating good parameters for a linear model can be hard sometimes and one should be very careful not to trust the results immediately. However, a Bayesian approach to the problem helps to include prior knowledge into the model and drive it toward a more stable and usable solution.

We saw ridge regression and Bayesian linear regression. We saw that, when the parameters have a Gaussian prior, then these two approaches are equivalent and very easy to compute.

Using a simple example, we saw that a standard regression can lead to completely over-fitted results and that the Bayesian approach solved the problem.

In the next chapter, we will look at more advanced models for dealing with clusters of data, called mixture models. These models make the assumption that the data is generated by a different group and the goal will be to automatically discover the group and reveal the hidden process behind it.

Probabilistic Mixture Models

7

We have seen an initial example of mixture models, namely the Gaussian mixture model, in which we had a finite number of Gaussians to represent a dataset. In this chapter, we will focus on more advanced examples of mixture models, going again from the Gaussian mixture model to the Latent Dirichlet Allocation. The reason for so many models is that we want to capture various aspects of the data that are not easily captured by a mixture of Gaussian.

In many cases, we will use the EM algorithm to find the parameters of the model from the data. Also, it appears that most of the mixture models can have intractable solutions and need solutions on approximate inferences.

The first type of model we will see is a mixture of simple distributions. The simple distribution can be a Gaussian, a Bernoulli, a Poisson, and so on. The principle is always the same but the applications are different. If Gaussian distributions are nice for capturing clouds of points, Bernoulli distributions can be efficient to analyze black and white images, for example, in handwritten recognition.

We will then relax one assumption of the mixture model and see a second type of model called mixture of experts, in which the chosen cluster is dependent on the data point. It can be seen as a first approach to probabilistic decision trees.

Finally, we will see a very powerful model called the **Latent Dirichlet Allocation (LDA)**, in which we relax another assumption of the mixture models. In mixture models, a point is supposed to have been generated by one cluster. In the LDA, it can belong to several clusters at the same time. This model has been successfully used in text analysis, among other things. It belongs to a family of mixed memberships models.

We will review the following elements in this chapter:

- Mixture models in general, with examples of several distributions
- Mixture of experts, when we assume clusters are dependent on the data points
- LDA when we assume a point belongs to several clusters

Mixture models

The mixture model is a model of a larger distribution family called latent variable models, in which some of the variables are not observed at all. The reason is usually to simplify the model by grouping all the variables into subgroups with a different meaning. Another reason is also to introduce a hidden process into the model, the real reason for the data generation process. In other words, we assume that we have a set of models and something hidden will select one of these models, and then generate a data point from the selected model.

When the data naturally exhibits clusters, it seems reasonable to say that each cluster is a small model.

The whole problem is then to find to what extent a submodel will participate in the data generation process and what the parameters for each sub model are. This is usually solved using the EM algorithm.

There are many ways to combine small models in order to make a bigger or more generic model. The approach generally used in mixture modeling is to give a proportion to each sub model, such that the sum of proportions is one. In other words, we build an additive model as follows:

$$p\left(x_i \mid \theta\right) = \sum_{i=1}^{K} \pi_k p_k\left(x_i \mid \theta\right)$$

In this, π_k is the proportion of each sub model. And each sub model is captured by the probability distribution p_k.

Of course, in this form, the sum of π_k is 1. Also, the proportions can be considered as random variables and the model can be extended in a Bayesian way. The model is therefore called a mixture model and the probability distribution p_k is called the base distribution.

There are, theoretically, no constraints on the form of the base distribution and, depending of the function, several types of model arise. In *Machine Learning: A Probabilistic Perspective*, the following taxonomy helps us to understand many popular models:

Name	Base distribution	Latent var. distribution	Notes
Mixture of Gaussian	Gaussian	Discrete	A Gaussian is chosen among K
Probabilistic PCA	Gaussian	Gaussian	
Probabilistic ICA	Gaussian	Laplace	Used for sparse coding
Latent Dirichlet Allocation	Discrete	Dirichlet	Used for text analysis

These are just a few examples to show that many models are possible based on the same principle. However, it does not mean they are all easy to solve and, in many cases, advanced algorithms will be necessary.

For example, the mixture of Gaussian model is defined as follows: we consider that each sub model is a Gaussian distribution (base distribution) and the latent variable distribution is discrete. For each distribution, we have a mean and a variance.

Sampling from such a model could give the following data set, for example:

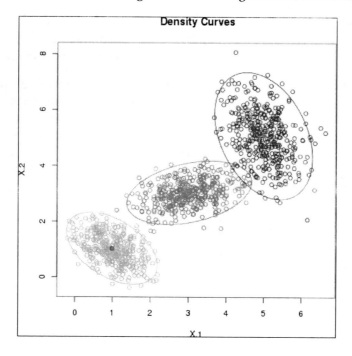

The base density is:

$$p(x_i \mid \theta, z_i = k) = N\left(x_i \mid \mu_k, \sigma_k^2\right)$$

And the latent variable distribution is a categorical distribution $\Pi = \left(\pi_1, \ldots, \pi_K\right)$.

The model is therefore:

$$p(x_i \mid \theta) = \sum_{i=1}^{K} \quad N\left(x_i \mid \mu_k, \sigma_k^2\right)$$

In the case of a multidimensional Gaussian, the variance σ_k^2 will be replaced by the covariance matrix Σ_k.

EM for mixture models

The standard way for fitting mixture models is the **EM** algorithm or **Expectation Maximization**. This algorithm was the focus of *Chapter 3, Learning Parameters*. So here, we just recall the basic principles of this algorithm again, to later show a Bernoulli mixture model.

A good package to use in R is `mixtools` to learn mixture models. A thorough presentation of this package is given in the Journal of Statistical Software, Oct 2009, Vol 32, Issue 6, *mixtools: An R Package for Analyzing Finite Mixture Models*.

The EM algorithm is a good choice for learning a mixture model. Indeed, in *Chapter 3, Learning Parameters*, we saw that when data is missing or even when variables are hidden (that is, all their respective data is missing), the EM algorithm will proceeds in two steps: first compute the expected value of the missing variables, so that to do as if the data is fully observed, and then maximize an objective function, usually the likelihood. Then, given the new set of parameters, the process is iterated again until some convergence criterion is reached.

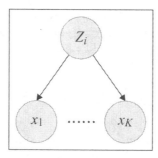

In the mixture model represented by the preceding graphical model, it is clear that the variable z is the latent variable and the x_i is observed. We usually adopt plate notation to give a comprehensive view of the data generation process as a graphical model and use the following graph:

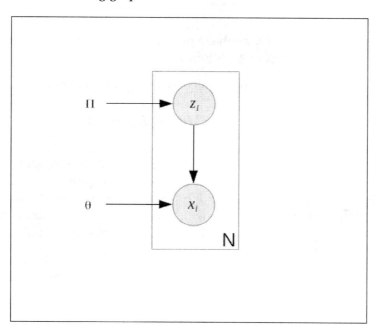

As in many probabilistic models, fitting the parameters can be solved by finding the set of parameters that maximizes the probability to generate the data. In other words, we aim at maximizing the log-likelihood of the model:

$$L(\theta) = \prod_{i=1}^{N} p(x_i \mid \theta) = \sum_{i=1}^{N} \log\left(\sum_{z_i}^{K} p(x_i, z_i \mid \theta)\right)$$

And that's where the problem is because the sum inside the log is hard to reduce and in many cases it is intractable. You will also note that this likelihood is written in terms of the observed data. So, if we follow the previous graphical model, we can write the complete log-likelihood by introducing the latent variables as follows:

$$L_c(\theta) = \sum_{i=1}^{N} \log p(x_i, z_i \mid \theta)$$

The EM algorithm will solve the problem of computing this likelihood, in which z is completely hidden, by performing the following two steps.

First of all, we define the **expected complete data log likelihood** by:

$$Q(\theta_t, \theta_{t-1}) = E(L_c(\theta) \mid Data\ \theta_{t-1})$$

This expectation is the expected complete data log likelihood computed from the parameters found in the previous step. Of course, at the beginning of the algorithm, the parameters are initialized to some arbitrary value. We saw in *Chapter 3, Learning Parameters* that this value can be anything, but choosing values at random can lead to a very long convergence time. Nevertheless, it has been proved that the EM algorithm converges for any value.

The E-step in the EM algorithm will compute this expected value — that is, the expected parameters given the data and the previous parameters.

Then the M-step will maximize this expectation given the newly found set of parameters θ that will solve the problem:

$$\theta_t = argmax_\theta Q(\theta_t, \theta_{t-1})$$

In the `mixtools` package, it is possible to fit a mixture of Gaussian using the function `normalmixEM`. Here is how to do so.

First, we generate a simple data set of two univariate Gaussian:

```
x1 ← rnorm(1000,-3,2)
x2 ← rnorm(850,3,1)
```

Then, we plot the result to see how they are empirically distributed using the `hist` function:

```
hist(c(x1,x2), breaks=100, col='red')
```

And we obtain the following figure, where we can easily identify the two clusters of data and see they are approximately distributed. Given that we use random generators, your result might be slightly different from what is shown in this book:

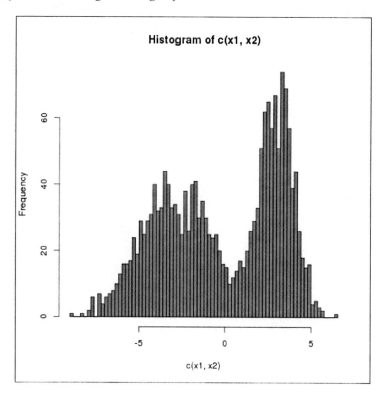

```
model ← normalmixEM( c(x1,x2) , lambda=.5, k=2)
```

This model should take between 30 to 40 iterations to run. We give an initial proportion of 50% to each class and set the number of clusters to 2.

In our results, we obtain the following parameters:

- The mixing proportions are 54.9% and 45.1%. This precisely corresponds to the proportion we gave to our data sets x1 and x2.

- The μ parameters are -2.85 and 3.01, which are extremely close to the initial values we gave too.

We can plot this histogram again with the Gaussian distributions superimposed on it:

```
hist(c(x1,x2),breaks=100,col='red',freq=F,ylim=c(0,0.4))
lines(x,dnorm(x,model$mu[1],model$sigma[1]), col='blue')
lines(x,dnorm(x,model$mu[2],model$sigma[2]), col='green')
```

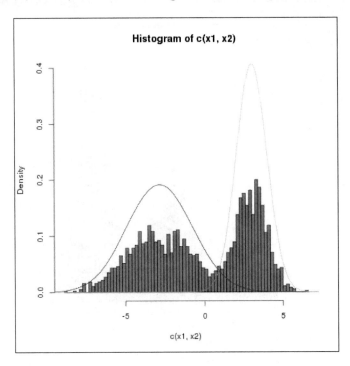

The result is obviously far off what we expected in terms of proportion. If we redraw it by adding the proportions now, we obtain the expected mixture distribution:

```
hist(c(x1,x2),breaks=100,col='red',freq=F)

lines(x,

  model$lambda[1]*dnorm(x,model$mu[1],model$sigma[1]) + model$lambda[2]*d
norm(x,model$mu[2],model$sigma[2]) ,

  lwd=3)
```

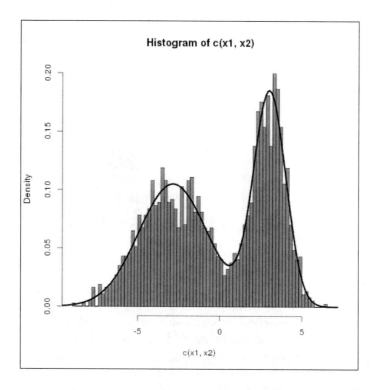

The number of clusters is very important and can change the results dramatically when not chosen properly. For example, if we try the following values, we end up with different results:

```
model <- normalmixEM(c(x1,x2), lambda=.5, k=3)
number of iterations= 774
model <- normalmixEM(c(x1,x2), lambda=.5, k=4)
WARNING! NOT CONVERGENT!
number of iterations= 1000
```

With three clusters, the EM algorithm still converges. With four clusters, we need to increase the number of iterations for the algorithm to converge. In fact, even with three clusters, the result is interesting if not surprising. Plotting the density function, we obtain:

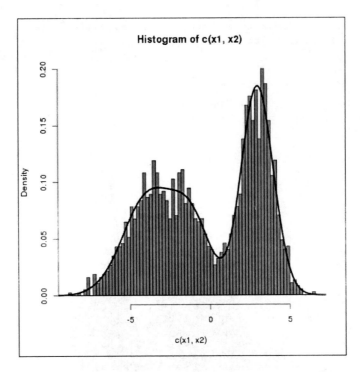

In this plot, we see that the second cluster is somehow attached to the first one. If you carefully look at the thick black line in the middle, you will see that the left-hand side distribution is not totally Gaussian. Inspecting the model parameters, we see that the means of the Gaussian are -3.74, -1.08, and 2.9. The middle one is indeed closer to the first cluster. The proportion is interesting: 38%, 15.4%, and 46.5%. So it seems the EM algorithm split the biggest cluster (1,000 points against 850) into 2 Gaussian to respect our choice of three clusters.

A slow convergence can sometimes be an indication that our hyperparameters are not totally adequate and more values should be explored.

Mixture of Bernoulli

The mixture of Bernoulli is another interesting problem. As we saw earlier, the graphical model to represent such a model is always the same. Only the probability distribution functions associated to each node change compared to the previous example. The mixture of Bernoulli finds applications in particular in analyzing black and white images, where an image is made of one Bernoulli variable for each pixel. Then the goal is to classify an image, that is, to say which value of the latent variable produced it, given some observed pixels.

For example, the following (very stylized) figure represents the letter A:

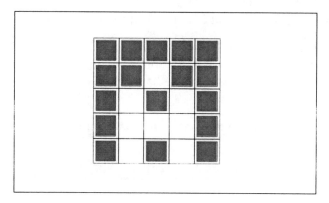

In a real application, we would use more pixels. But the idea of the application is to associate the value of pixels to each value of the latent variable, each one representing a different letter. This is a simple model for character recognition.

The distribution of a Bernoulli variable is:

$$p\left(x\,|\,\theta\right) = \theta^{x}\left(1-\theta\right)^{1-x}$$

Now, let's say we have D Bernoulli variables. Each Bernoulli variable is parameterized by one parameter θ_i. So the likelihood of such a model can be written as:

$$p\left(X\,|\,\theta\right) = \prod_{i=1}^{D}\theta_i^{x_i}\left(1-\theta_i\right)^{\left(1-x_i\right)}$$

Here, $X = (x_1, \ldots, x_D)$ and $\theta = (\theta_1, \ldots, \theta_D)$.

If we introduce the mixture of all the variables then the joint distribution can be written as:

$$p(X \mid \theta\pi) = \sum_{i=1}^{K} \pi_K p(x \mid \theta_k)$$

Here, $\pi = (\pi_1, \dots \pi_D)$ are the mixing parameters and the distribution p is inside as:

$$p(x \mid \theta_k) = \prod_{i=1}^{D} \theta_{k,i}^{x_i} \left(1 - \theta_{k,i}\right)^{1-x_i}$$

This is in fact the same distribution as before but for a case k only.

In order to fit this model, we need now to find the log-likelihood and, as expected, its expression will not be suitable for a direct optimization. The reason is, as usual, that we introduce latent variables for which we have no observations and we therefore need to use an EM algorithm.

The log-likelihood is taken from the main joint distribution:

$$\log p(x \mid \theta\pi) = \sum_{n=1}^{N} \log\left(\sum_{i=1}^{K} \pi_k p(x_i \mid \theta_i)\right)$$

This is a pretty standard way of computing the log-likelihood. And, as is usually the case for mixture models, the sum inside the log cannot be pushed out. So we end up with a quite complex expression to minimize.

Now we introduce the latent variable z into the model. It has a categorical distribution with K parameters, such that:

$$p(z \mid \pi) = \prod_{k=1}^{K} \pi_k^{z_k}$$

And the joint distribution with x is as follows:

$$p(x \mid z\theta) = \prod_{k=1}^{K} p(x \mid \theta_k)^{z_k}$$

As before with the Gaussian mixture, we will write the complete data log-likelihood. This likelihood is what we would optimize if the data set were complete — that is, without latent variables:

$$\log p\left(X,Z \mid \theta\pi\right) = \sum_{n=1}^{N}\sum_{k=1}^{K} z_{n,k}\left(\log \pi_k\right.$$
$$\left. + \sum_{i=1}^{D}\left[x_{n,i}\log\theta_{k,i} + \left(1 - x_{n,i}\right)\log\left(1 - \theta_{k,i}\right)\right]\right)$$

In this (very long) expression, we consider X and Z to be matrices, so in fact we use the design matrix notation, where each row vector of X (resp. Z) is one set of observations of each variable x_i (resp. z).

Using the Bayes formula, we can calculate the expectation of the complete-data log-likelihood with respect to the distribution of the latent variable. This step is necessary for the E-step of the EM algorithm, where we want to complete the data set:

$$E_z\left(\log p\left(X,Z \mid \theta\pi\right)\right) = \sum_{n=1}^{N}\sum_{k=1}^{K} E\left(z_{n,k}\right)\left(\log \pi_k\right.$$
$$\left. + \sum_{i=1}^{D}\left[x_{n,i}\log\theta_{k,i} + \left(1 - x_{n,i}\right)\log\left(1 - \theta_{k,i}\right)\right]\right)$$

And the expected value of the latent variable is:

$$E\left(z_{n,k}\right) = \frac{\pi_k p\left(x_i \mid \theta_k\right)}{\sum_{j=1}^{K}\pi_j p\left(x_n \mid \theta_j\right)}$$

In a sense, this is not surprising because in the end we need to compute the ratio of z_i for each subset of the dataset in which it appears after the posterior computations.

Finally, in the M-step, we can derive the complete-data log-likelihood with respect to the parameters θ_k and π and set it equal to zero. We obtain the following estimators:

$$\theta_k = \frac{1}{N_k}\sum_{n=1}^{N} E\left(z_{n,k}\right)x_n$$

$$\pi_k = \frac{N_k}{N}$$

Here, $N_k = \sum_{n=1}^{N} E\left(z_{n,k}\right)$.

The EM algorithm will alternate between computing the expectation of z and the new values for the parameters θ and π until convergence.

[More details about the derivation can be found in *Pattern Recognition and Machine Learning*, Christopher M. Bishop, Springer, 2007]

This model can be extended and the same principles applied to other types of distribution—for example, a mixture of Poisson or Gamma. On the other hand, the mixture of Bernoulli can be extended to the multinomial case with the same type of derivation.

In all those models, however, we consider that we have one model for all the data point space. In other words, we somehow use the same model for the whole support of the distribution.

One extension is to consider that each subspace has its own model and therefore the choice of the sub model made by the latent variable is dependent on the data points. In *Adaptive mixtures of local experts*, Jacobs, R.A., Jordan, M.I, Nowlan, S.J., and Hinton, G.E. (1991) in Neural Computation, 3, 79-87, such a model is presented. We give a brief review of this interesting model in its simple form.

Mixture of experts

The idea behind mixture of experts is to use a set of linear regressions for each sub space of the original data space and combine them with weighting functions that will successively give weight to each linear regression.

Consider the following example dataset, which we generate with the following toy code:

```
x1=runif(40,0,10)
x2=runif(40,10,20)

e1 = rnorm(20,0,2)
```

```
e2 = rnorm(20,0,3)


y1 = 1+2.5*x1 + e1
y2 = 35+-1.5*x2 + e2


xx=c(x1,x2)
yy=c(y1,y2)
```

Plotting the result, and doing a simple linear regression on it, gives the following:

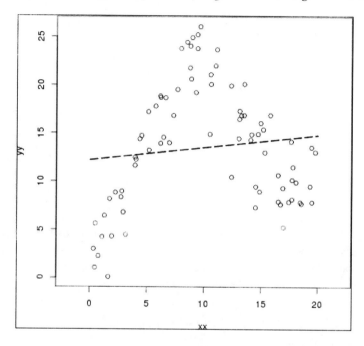

Obviously, the linear regression does not capture the behavior of the data at all. It barely captures a general trend in the data that more or less averages the data set.

The idea of mixture of experts is to have several sub models within a bigger model—for example, having several regression lines, as the following graph:

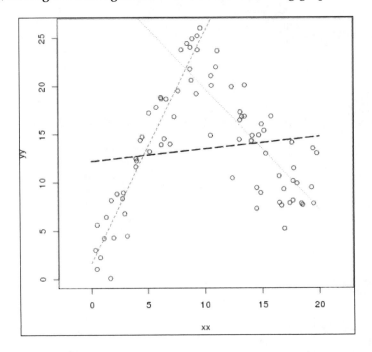

In this graph, the red and green lines seems to better represent the data set. However, the model needs to choose when to choose each one. Again, a mixture model could be a solution, except that, in this case, we want the mixture to be dependent on the data points. So the graphical model will be a bit different:

$$p\left(y_i \mid x_i, z_i, \theta\right) = N\left(y_i \mid w_k^T x_i, \sigma_k^2\right)$$

This is the linear model as we know it. Next we introduce the dependence of the latent variable to the data points with:

$$p\left(z_i \mid x_i \theta\right) = Mult\left(z_i \mid S\left(V^T x_i\right)\right)$$

Here, $S(.)$ is, for example, a sigmoid function. The function $p(z_i \mid x_i\theta)$ is usually called the **gating function**.

The graphical model associated with such a model is quite different now because it introduces a dependency between the latent variable and the observations:

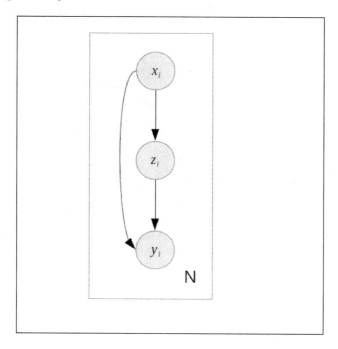

In general, mixture of experts models uses a softmax gating function such that:

$$f(x) = \frac{\exp\left(\beta^T x\right)}{\sum_{n=1}^{k} \exp\left(\beta^T x\right)}$$

The EM algorithm is usually a good algorithm to fit such a model. For example, the `mixtools` package includes a function `hmeME` to fit mixture of experts models. At the time of writing, this function is limited to two clusters.

The combination of all the gating functions requires us to sum to one at each point; for example, in our example we could use two sigmoids with the following effect:

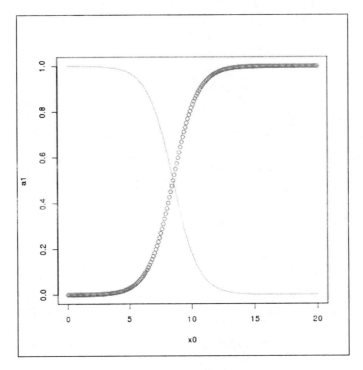

And such a combination could give a final model that better interprets the initial data set, such as this graph:

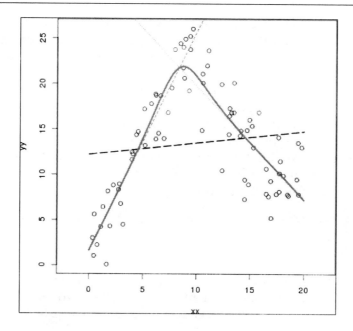

We recommend the reader develop his or her own EM algorithm to fit such models and try different types of gating functions.

Techniques such as shrinkage or using a Bayesian approach on the parameters could be useful to avoid over-fitting too, which can be problematic when the number of sub models grows quickly.

Latent Dirichlet Allocation

The last model we want to present in this book is called the Latent Dirichlet Allocation. It is a generative model that can be represented as a graphical model. It's based on the same idea as the mixture model, with one notable exception. In this model, we assume that the data points might be generated by a combination of clusters and not just one cluster at a time, as was the case before.

The LDA model is primarily used in text analysis and classification. Let's consider that a text document is composed of words making sentences and paragraphs. To simplify the problem, we can say that each sentence or paragraph is about one specific topic, such as science, animals, sports, and so on. Topics can also be more specific, such as *cats* or *European soccer*. Therefore, there are words that are more likely to come from specific topics. For example, the word *cat* is likely to come from the topic *cats*. The word *stadium* is likely to come from the topic *European soccer*. However, the word *ball* should come with a higher probability from the topic *European soccer*, but it is not unlikely to come from the topic *cats*, because cats like to play with balls too. So it seems the word *ball* might belong to two topics at the same time with a different degree of certainty.

Other words such as *table* will certainly belong equally to both topics and presumably to others. They are very generic. Unless, of course, we introduce another topic such as *furniture*.

A document is a collection of words, so a document can have complex relationships to a set of topics. But, in the end, it is more likely we will see words coming from the same topic or the same topics within a paragraph, and to some extent in the document.

In general, we model a document with a bag-of-words model that is, we consider a document to be a randomly generated set of words, using a specific distribution over the words. If this distribution is uniform over all the words, then the document will be purely random without a specific meaning. However, if this distribution has a specific form, with more probability mass to related words, then the collection of words generated by this model will have a meaning. Of course, generating documents is not really the application we have in mind for such a model. What we are interested in is the analysis of documents, their classification, and automatic understanding.

The LDA model

Let's say z_i is a categorical variable (in other words, a histogram) representing the probability of appearance of all words from a dictionary.

Usually, in this kind of model, we restrict ourselves to long words and remove the small words such as and, to, but, the, a, and so on. These words are usually called **stop words**.

Let w_j be the jth word in a document. A document generating model could be represented with the following graphical model:

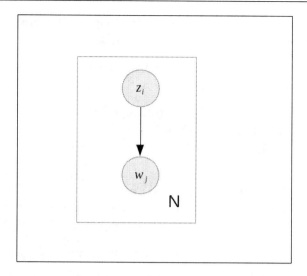

Let θ be a distribution over topics, then we can extend this model by choosing which kind of topic will be selected at any time and then generate a word out of it.

Therefore, the variable z_i now becomes the variable z_{ij}, which is the topic i selected for the word j. The graphical model is extended as follows:

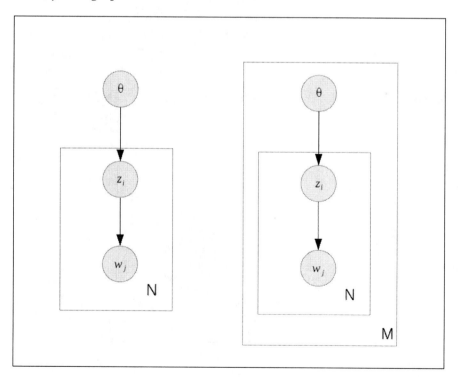

We can go even further and decide we want to model a collection of documents, which seems natural if we consider we have a big dataset.

Assuming that documents are *i.i.d*, we can draw the following graphical model again, in which we capture M documents (on the right in the earlier figure).

And because the distribution on θ is categorical, we want to be Bayesian about it, mainly because it will help to model (not to over-fit) and because we consider the selection of topics for a document to be a random process in itself.

Moreover, we want to apply the same treatment to the word variable by having a Dirichlet prior. This prior is used to avoid non-observed words having a zero probability. It smooths the distribution of words per topic. A uniform Dirichlet prior will induce a uniform prior distribution on all the words.

The final graphical model is given by the following figure:

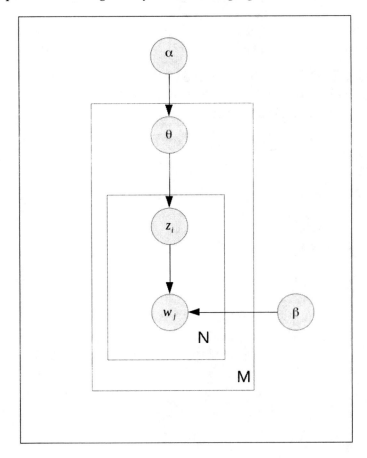

This is quite a complex graphical model but techniques have been developed to fit the parameters and use this model.

So, if we follow this graphical model carefully, we have a process that generates documents based on a certain set of topics:

- α chooses the set of topics for a document
- From θ we generate a topic z_{ij}
- From this topic, we generate a word w_j

In this model, only the words are observable. All the other variables will have to be determined without observation, exactly like in the other mixture models. So documents are represented as random mixtures over latent topics, in which each topic is represented as a distribution over words.

The distribution of a topic mixture based on this graphical model can be written as:

$$p(\theta, z, w \mid \alpha\beta) = p(\theta \mid \alpha) \prod_{i=1}^{N} p(z_i \mid \theta) p(w_i \mid z_i, \beta)$$

You see in this formula that for each word we select a topic, hence the product from 1 to N.

Integrating over θ, and summing over z, the marginal distribution of a document is as follows:

$$p(w \mid \alpha\beta) = \int p(\theta \mid \alpha) \left(\prod_{i=1}^{N} \sum_{z_i} p(z_i \mid \theta) p(w_i \mid z_i\beta) \right) d\theta$$

The final distribution can be obtained by taking the product of marginal distributions of single documents, so as to get the distribution over a collection of documents (assuming documents are independently and identically distributed). Here, D is the collection of documents:

$$p(D \mid \alpha\beta) = \prod_{d=1}^{M} \int p(\theta_d \mid \alpha) \left(\prod_{i=1}^{N_d} \sum_{z_{d,i}} p(z_{d,i} \mid \theta_d) p(w_{d,i} \mid z_{d,i}\beta) \right) d\theta_d$$

The main problem to solve now is how to compute the posterior distribution over θ and z given a document. By applying the Bayes formula we know that:

$$p(\theta, z \mid w\alpha\beta) = \frac{p(\theta, z, w \mid \alpha, \beta)}{p(w \mid \alpha\beta)}$$

Unfortunately, this is intractable because of the normalization factor at the denominator. The original paper on LDA therefore refers to a technique called **variational inference**, which aims at transforming a complex Bayesian inference problem into a simpler approximation which can be solved as a (convex) optimization problem. This technique is the third approach to Bayesian inference and has been used on many other problems. In the next section, we briefly review the principles of variational inference and, finally, we will show an example in R to conclude this section.

Variational inference

The main idea in variational inference is to consider a family of lower bounds indexed by variational parameters and optimize on those parameters to find the tightest lower bound. Practically speaking, the idea is to approximate a complicated distribution we wish to evaluate by a simpler distribution such that the distance (or any suitable metric between the distributions) can be minimized with a convex optimization procedure. The reason we want things to be convex is essentially because convex problems have a global minimum.

In general, a good approximation for a graphical model consists in simplifying the graph of the model by decoupling variables. In practice, we remove edges.

In the LDA model, the proposed variational problem is done by decoupling the variables θ and β.

The resulting graphical model after decoupling no longer shows the connection between θ and z_i but includes new free variational parameters. The final distribution is given by:

$$q(\theta z \mid \gamma \phi) = q(\theta \mid \gamma) \prod_{i=1}^{N} q(z_i \mid \varphi_i)$$

Here, γ is a Dirichlet variable and Φ a multinomial.

The optimization problem requires a way to calculate some distance or discrepancy between the simplified distribution and the real distribution.

This is usually done by using the Kullback-Leibler divergence between the two distributions. The optimization problem is now to find (γ, ϕ) such that:

$$\left(\gamma^*, \varphi^*\right) = argmin_{(\gamma, \varphi)} D\left(q(\theta, z \mid \gamma, \varphi) \| p(\theta, z \mid w, \alpha, \beta)\right)$$

Many optimization algorithms are able to solve this problem.

The fitting of the parameters of the model can be done again using the EM algorithm. However, as in inference, the E-step is intractable but can be solved with the variational approximation of this problem.

The E-step consists in finding the values for the variational parameters for each document. Then the M-step consists in maximizing the lower bound of the log-likelihood with respect to the parameters α and β. The steps are repeated until convergence of the lower bound on the log-likelihood.

Examples

We will use the `RtextTools` and `topicmodels` packages. The second one contains an implementation of the LDA model as described before.

First we load some data:

```
data(NYTimes)

data ← NYTimes[ samples(1:3100, size=1000,replace=F) ]
```

The resulting `data.frame` contains `titles` and `subject` and an associated `topic.code`. This dataset contains headlines from the New York Times.

Then we create a matrix suitable for the `LDA()` function in the `topicmodels` package:

```
matrix ← create_matrix(cbind(as.vector(data$Title),as.
vector(data$Subject)), language="english," removeNumbers=TRUE,
stemWords=TRUE)
```

Next, we set up the number of topics. This is computed by looking at the number of unique `topic.code` in the original data set. This data set has been specially compiled for this task:

```
k <- length(unique(data$Topic.Code))
```

Finally, we run the learning algorithm using the variational EM algorithm. This function also provide a Gibbs sampling method to solve the same problem:

```
lda <- LDA(matrix, k)
```

The result is a topic model with 27 topics, as expected. Let's see this in detail. The returned object is an S4 object (so you will notice we use the @ notation in R).

Let's take the first document and look at its posterior distribution over the topics:

```
print(lda@gamma[1,])
```

```
 [1] 0.649978052 0.004191364 0.004191364 0.004191364 0.004191364
0.004191364 0.004191364 0.004191364 0.004191364 0.004191364 0.004191364
0.004191364 0.004191364 0.004191364 0.004191364 0.004191364
```

```
[17] 0.004191364 0.004191364 0.115045483 0.004191364 0.004191364
0.004191364 0.134383733 0.004191364 0.004191364 0.004191364 0.004191364
```

We see that the first topic has a higher probability. We can plot this to view it better:

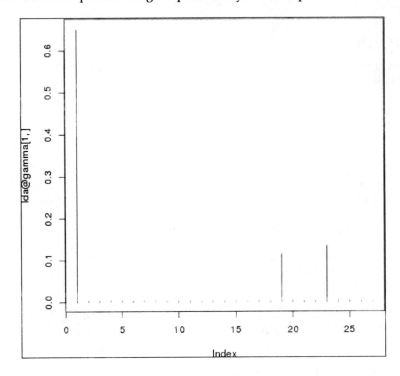

And we will also look at an average graph over all the documents by doing:

```
plot(colSums(lda@gamma)/nrow(lda@gamma),t='h')
```

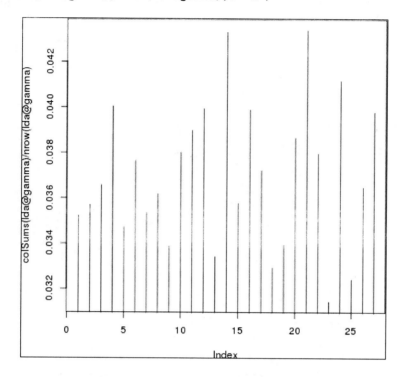

From there, we can see the distribution over the topics is clearly not uniform, which would have been really surprising.

So we have a simple way to extract the most probable topic from each document. Note that, in the case of the first document, one topic was highly probable and two others appeared too. The rest were insignificant.

We can, for example, search for the number of documents that have two or more topics with a probability higher than 10%:

```
sum(sapply( 1:nrow(lda@gamma), function(i) sum(lda@gamma[i,]>0.1) > 1))
```

We find 649 over 1,000 documents. However, if we look at intervals of 10% from 0% to 100%, we see that this number drops quickly. So it seems that our data set has a lot of documents that identify themselves to only one topic at a time. The following graph shows this progression:

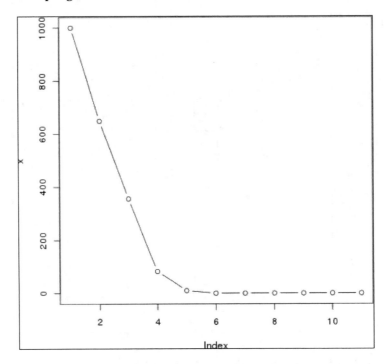

For example, at 30% only a couple of hundred documents still share their topics among at least two topics. Then the number drops. All sorts of analysis can be done on such a collection, such as finding the words belonging to a topic.

Summary

In this last chapter, we saw more advanced probabilistic graphical models, whose solution is not easy to compute with standard tools such as the junction tree algorithm. This chapter set out to show that the graphical model framework can still be used even if one has to develop a special algorithm for each model. Indeed, in the LDA model, the solution to the variational problem appeared by looking at the graph of the original LDA and by transforming this graph, thus leading to a better approximation of the initial problem. So, even if the final algorithm does not use the graph directly like a junction tree algorithm would do, the solution came from the graph anyway.

This chapter proved how powerful probabilistic graphical models can be, and all the possibilities and new models that can be created from simpler models.

Indeed, each of these models can again be extended either by combining them—for example, in the mixture of experts model. In this model, each expert function could be replaced by another mixture of experts model, creating a hierarchical mixture of experts. This is a probabilistic version of the decision tree but with smooth transitions and an increased ability to deal with uncertainty.

We have finally reached the end of our journey into the world of probabilistic graphical models. But, as with all journeys, it is just a start and we encourage the reader to look for all the R packages dedicated to graphical models and to write his or her own algorithms. Following the graphs and the generic recipes found in this book, it is possible to go way beyond the standard models and solutions we presented here; the only limit is your imagination.

Appendix

References

The following references were used while writing this book. We encourage those of you who want to go further into the field of probabilistic graphical models and Bayesian modeling to read at least some of them.

Many of our examples and presentations of algorithms took inspiration from these books and papers.

Books on the Bayesian theory

- Gelman, A., Carlin, J.B., Stern, H.S., Dunson, D.B, Vehtari, A., and Rubin, D.B.. *Bayesian Data Analysis*, 3rd Edition. CRC Press. 2013. This is a reference book on Bayesian modeling covering topics from the most fundamental aspects to the most advanced, with the focus on modeling and also on computations.

- Robert, C.P.. *The Bayesian Choice: From Decision-Theoretic Foundations to Computational Implementation*. Springer. 2007. This is a beautiful presentation of the Bayesian paradigm with many examples. The book is more theoretical but has a rigorous presentation of many aspects of the Bayesian paradigm.

- McGrayne, Sharon Bertsch. *The Theory That Would Not Die*. Yale University Press. 2011. This talks about how Bayes' rule cracked the Enigma code, hunted down Russian submarines, and emerged triumphant from two centuries of controversy. It is a brilliantly written history of Bayes' rule going from the seminal paper of Thomas Bayes to the latest advances in the 21st century.

Books on machine learning

- Murphy, K.P.. *Machine Learning: A Probabilistic Perspective*. The MIT Press. 2012. This is a book on machine learning in general with a lot of algorithms. It covers more than just graphical models and Bayesian models. It is one of the best references.

- Bishop, C.M. *Pattern Recognition and Machine Learning*. Springer. 2007. This is one of the best books on machine learning, covering many aspects and going through many details of the implementation of each algorithm.

- Barber, D.. *Bayesian Reasoning and Machine Learning*. Cambridge University Press. 2012. This is another excellent reference book covering many aspects of machine learning with a specific focus on Bayesian models.

- Robert, C.P.. *Monte Carlo Methods in Statistics*. 2009. (`http://arxiv.org/pdf/0909.0389.pdf`) This is an excellent paper on the Monte Carlo methods, and it is very pedagogical.

- Koller, D. and Friedman, N.. *Probabilistic Graphical Models: Principles and Techniques*. The MIT Press. 2009. This is the most complete and advanced book on probabilistic graphical models. It covers all aspects of the domain. This book is very dense, with thorough details on many algorithms related to PGM and useful demonstrations. Probably the best book on PGM.

- Casella, G. and Berger, R.L.. *Statistical Inference*, 2nd Edition. Duxbury. 2002: This is a reference book on standard statistics with many detailed demonstrations. It's a book that anyone doing statistics should read.

- Hastie, T., Tibshirani, R., and Friedman, J.. *The Elements of Statistical Learning: Data Mining, Inference, and Prediction*. Springer. 2013: This is a book best-seller and covers the most important aspects of machine learning from a statistical point of view.

Papers

- Jacobs, R.A., Jordan, M.I, Nowlan, S.J., and Hinton, G.E. *Adaptive mixtures of local experts*. 1991 in Neural Computation, 3, 79-87: This is the reference paper on mixture of experts as seen in *Chapter 7, Probabilistic Mixture Models*.

- Blei, David M., Ng, Andrew, Y, Jordan, Michael, I. *Latent Dirichlet Allocation*. January 2003, Journal of Machine Learning Research 3 (4–5), p993–1022: This is a reference paper on the LDA model as seen in *Chapter 7, Probabilistic Mixture Models*.

Index

A

ancestral sampling 128
arm package 195

B

basic sampling algorithms
  about 129
  standard distributions 129-133
Bayesian Linear models
  about 176
  graphical model 179-181
  implementation, in R 184-188
  over-fitting 176-179
  packages 194
  packages, in R 195
  posterior distribution 181-184
  stable implementation 188-194
Bayesian Naive Bayes 104-106
Bayesian theory
  references 227
bayesm package 194
Bayes' rule
  about 11
  conditional probability 12
  example 13-19
  formula, interpreting 13
Bernoulli distribution 108
Beta-Binomial
  about 106-111
  posterior distribution, with conjugacy
    property 112, 113
  prior distribution 111, 112
  values, selecting for Beta parameters 113
Binomial distribution 110

bnlearn R package
  about 65
  URL 65

C

cluster nodes 54
conjugacy property 112, 113
continuous random variable 36

D

Dirichlet distribution 105
discrete random variable 36
discrete sepal width (dsw) 74
d-separation 37

E

empirical distribution
  relating, to model distribution 79-81
Expectation Maximization (EM) algorithm
  about 70
  applying, to graphical models 93, 94
  derivation 91, 92
  for mixture models 200-206
  principles 90
  with hidden variables 88

G

gating function 213
Gaussian mixture model
  about 115
  defining 116-122
  example 115
generative models 70